Luftwaffe
Handbook
1939-1945

Luftwaffe
Handbook
1939-1945

Alfred Price FRHistS

LONDON
IAN ALLAN LTD

First published 1977

ISBN o 7110 0632 6

Published by Ian Allan Ltd, Shepperton, Surrey
Photoset, printed and bound in the United Kingdom by
Redwood Burn Limited, Trowbridge & Esher

Contents

Preface

In writing this my purpose has been to produce a basic reference manual on the *Luftwaffe*, to provide the reader with an insight into the organisation and working of that force. This book is not intended as a substitute for any of the previous works written on the subject but rather as a supplement to them, to answer questions on points which in the past have usually been omitted from detailed discussion. Some major aspects of the *Luftwaffe* have received less than their fair share of coverage: one such is the working of the *Flak* arm, which at the beginning of the Second World War engaged almost two-thirds of the man-power strength of the *Luftwaffe*; another is pilot training, on which the effectiveness of the flying units ultimately depended; and a third is that of the tactics employed by the various types of fighter and bomber unit. In each case I have tried to make good these omissions.

In putting this book together I have had much help from many good friends, in particular Hanfried Schliephake and Goetz Bergander in Germany. Mike Brook produced the diagrams.

This is the sort of book I should like to have had when I first began my serious research into the Luftwaffe fourteen years ago. Had it been available then, my task would have been much easier.

Uppingham
Rutland

Alfred Price
September 1976

I
The High Command

The Air Ministry

The *Luftwaffe* was directed from the *Reichsluftfahrt Ministerium* (Air Ministry), which had a dual function. Firstly, there was the *Oberkommando der Luftwaffe* (*Luftwaffe* High Command), concerned purely with the military direction of the air force; secondly, there was the office of the *Reichsminister der Luftfahrt* (State Minister for Air), which dealt with ministerial problems, long-term administration, financial control, civil aviation and, until 1944, aircraft production. Almost until the end of the war Hermann Goering headed both sections, with the titles of *Oberbefehlshaber der Luftwaffe* (Commander in Chief of the Air Force) and State Minister for Air.

The *Oberkommando der Luftwaffe* was divided into several numbered *Abteilungen* (Directorates), of which the more important were: 1 – Operations, 2 – Organisation, 3 – Training, 4 – Movements, 5 – Intelligence, 6 – Equipment, 8 – Historical and 9 – Personnel. Of these Directorates Nos 1, 3, and 5 came under the control of the Chief of the Operations Staff; he was responsible not only for operations but also for all basic decisions relating to the implementation of the air strategy as laid down by the Chief of the General Staff. The 8th Directorate (Historical) came directly under the Chief of the General Staff. The remainder of the major Directorates, Nos 2, 4, 6 and 9, came under the *Generalquartiermeister* (Quartermaster General). In addition to the Directorates there were several Inspectorates, which came under the Chief of the General Staff. These dealt with specific flying subjects such as fighter, ground attack, flight safety, etc.

'Robinson' and 'Kurfuerst'

For the greater part of the war the *Oberkommando der Luftwaffe* was split into two parts, a forward echelon and a rear echelon. The forward echelon comprised the Chief of the General Staff, the Operations Staff, the Director General of Signals, the Director of Training and part of the Intelligence Department. This echelon was code-named '*Robinson*' and was situated close to Hitler's headquarters; the latter was located at various places during the war, including Winniza, Goldap, Rosengarten, Insterburg and Berchtesgarden. The rear echelon was code-named '*Kurfuerst*' and comprised the other departments of the High Command; it was situated in and around Berlin. '*Robinson*' and '*Kurfuerst*' kept in close touch with each other by means of liaison officers and an excellent communications service.

There were two daily conferences at which the affairs of the *Luftwaffe* were decided. The more important was the afternoon meeting at Hitler's headquarters, presided over by the *Fuehrer* and attended by the Chiefs of Staffs of all three services; there the conduct and progress of the war as a whole were discussed, and decisions of the highest importance taken. The other conference took place at '*Robinson*' each morning and was chaired by the Chief of the *Luftwaffe* General Staff; there the force's operations on the various fronts and the decisions taken at the previous afternoon's *Fuehrer* Conference were discussed, and the necessary orders issued. Operational orders were sent from '*Robinson*' direct to the *Luftflotten* commanders.

The Luftflotte

At the beginning of the war almost all operational flying units of the *Luftwaffe* were divided between four *Luftflotten* (Air Fleets): *Luftflotte 1*, under General der Flieger Kesselring, had its headquarters in Berlin and covered northern and eastern Germany; *Luftflotte 2* (Felmy), headquarters at Brunswick, covered north-western Germany; *Luftflotte 3* (Sperrle), headquarters at Munich, covered south-western Germany; and *Luftflotte 4*, under General der Flieger Loehr, headquarters at Vienna, covered south-eastern Germany, Austria and Czechoslovakia. These *Luftflotten* were in fact self-contained and balanced air forces, each with its own fighter, bomber, reconnaissance, ground attack and other units; they were thus akin to the RAF or USAAF overseas Commands or Air Forces, rather than to the RAF home Commands which were organised functionally to operate in specific roles. As the Germans occupied more and more territory during the early part of the war, the areas covered by the original *Luftflotten* were extended far beyond their original boundaries. To prevent over-extension, during the course of the war three new *Luftflotten* were formed: *Luftflotte 5*, covering Norway, Finland and northern Russia; *Luftflotte 6*, covering central Russia; and *Luftflotte Reich*, responsible for all home air defence fighter and *Flak* units.

The Luftgau and the Fliegerkorps

During its expansion in the 1930s the *Luftwaffe* had been organised to exploit the great potential mobility of its flying units, so that forces could be concentrated rapidly at points at the front dictated by the military situation. To make it easier for flying units to move between bases within their *Luftflotte* area, they were freed of their administrative and supply organisations. The area of responsibility of each *Luftflotte* was sub-divided into several *Luftgaue* (Air Zones), each with a headquarters responsible for the provision of men for administrative, supply and second-line* technical tasks at the airfields within their

* Second-line servicing: those tasks requiring more men or equipment than were available to the normal flying unit.

domain. Thus the *Luftgau* provided the necessary 'hotel facilities' at the airfields, to enable incoming flying units to go into action from their new bases with a minimum of delay. An interesting point to note is that when a flying *Gruppe* took up residence at an airfield, its *Kommandeur* automatically took precedence over all other officers stationed there.

While the *Luftgau* organisation was responsible within its set area for all administrative matters, the parallel organisation for operational purposes was the *Fliegerkorps* (Air Corps). Typically a *Fliegerkorps* operated between 300 and 750 aircraft of all types, its strength depending upon the importance of its area and the nature of the operations it was called upon to fly. Usually a *Fliegerkorps* was subordinated to the *Luftflotte* covering the area, though sometimes the former did operate autonomously.

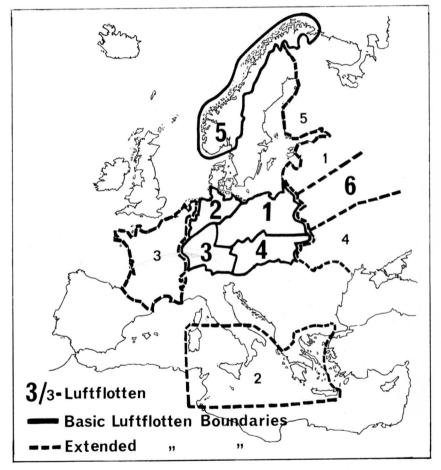

3/3-Luftflotten

▬▬ Basic Luftflotten Boundaries

▬ ▬ ▬Extended   „   „

The operational areas of the various *Luftflotten* in the spring of 1943. The original home *Luftflotten* boundaries are drawn in hard outline, and the extended *Luftflotten* boundaries in dashed outline.

During the pre-war expansionary phase of the *Luftwaffe* numerous well-equipped main bases, *Fliegerhorste*, were built.
Amongst the permanent facilities were large maintenance hangars (*top*), here seen at Schleswig, and air traffic control buildings (*above*), at Finsterwalde./*via Hanfried Schliephake*

After the initial victories the *Luftwaffe* set up a large number of operational bases, *Einsatzhafen*, in the occupied territories. These bases were characterised by the dispersal and camouflage of their limited facilities. (*above right*) a semi-revetted individual hangarette at Chartres in northern France, housing a Junkers 88; (*right*) a Messerschmitt 109F standing outside a hangarette camouflaged to look like a barn, at a fighter airfield in northern France./*via Hanfried Schliephake*

2
The Flying Units

The Staffel

The *Staffel*, with a nominal strength of nine aircraft, was the lowest grade of flying formation within the organisation of the *Luftwaffe*. Commanded by a *Staffelkapitaen*, usually an Oberleutnant or Hauptmann, members of its flying personnel would supervise the technical and signals branches as secondary duties. The *Staffel* usually had a few vehicles allocated to it, and a mobile repair shop to carry out minor repairs to the aircraft. The number of flying personnel in a *Staffel* naturally depended on the type of aircraft it operated; between ten (in the case of single-seat fighters) and more than forty (in the case of multi-engined bombers). The number of ground personnel in a *Staffel* varied from 150 (in the case of single-engined fighters) to 80 (in the case of multi-engined bombers); the latter's ground staff was smaller because much of its servicing and administration was done for it by attached units provided by the local *Luftgau* command. During the war the aircraft strength of the *Staffel* gradually rose to a maximum of sixteen, with corresponding rises in the number of aircrew and ground personnel.

The Gruppe

The *Gruppe* was the basic flying unit for operational and administrative purposes. When orders were given for moves of flying units, the recipients were usually *Gruppen*. Normally one complete *Gruppe* occupied a single airfield, though sometimes there would be more; occasionally individual *Staffeln* might be detached from their parent *Gruppe*, for operational reasons or to re-equip. Initially the *Gruppe* comprised three *Staffeln*, and a *Stab* (headquarters flight) with three more, making a total of thirty aircraft in all. By the mid-war period many fighter *Gruppen* operated a fourth *Staffel*, however, and this, with the sixteen-aircraft *Staffel* establishment, brought the strength of some *Gruppen* to sixty-seven aircraft.

The *Gruppe* commander carried the title of *Kommandeur* and was usually a Hauptmann or a Major; under his command he had an adjutant, specialist technical officers, and a medical officer. The total personnel strength of a

Pictured at the controls of his Heinkel
111 is Hauptmann Hans George Baetcher,
the Kommandeur of *I. Gruppe* of
Kampfgeschwader 100; the rank insignia
can be seen on the right arm of his flying
suit. On his helmet he wears the
standard issue aircrew sunglasses and
above them clear lensed goggles. It is
just possible to make out the microphone
(*Kehlkopfmikrophon*) strapped round
his throat; the standard German oxygen
mask did not contain a microphone and was
usually worn only for flights at high
altitudes./*Baetcher*

Gruppe varied between 35 and 150 aircrew, and 300 and 515 groundcrew.

The Geschwader

The *Geschwader* was the largest German flying unit to have a fixed nominal strength. Initially it comprised three *Gruppen*, with ninety aircraft, and a *Stab* flight with four, making a total of ninety-four. Later in the war a fourth, *Ergaenzungs*, *Gruppe* was added to each bomber *Geschwader* to provide operational training for crews before they moved to the front-line *Gruppen*; later still some *Geschwader* operated a fifth *Gruppe*, though this practice did not last long. Originally it had been intended that the component *Gruppen* of each *Geschwader* should operate together from adjacent airfields, but under the stress of war this arrangement soon broke down.

The *Geschwader* commander held the title of *Kommodore*, and was usually a Major, Oberstleutnant or Oberst; his staff included an adjutant, an operations officer, an Intelligence officer, a navigation officer, technical officers, a signals officer, and such other specialist officers as the nature of the unit's task might dictate.

Designations of Flying Units

Within a *Geschwader* the aircraft were usually assigned to a single role, for example *Jagdgeschwader* (abbreviated to *JG*), fighters; *Nachtjagd-* (*NJG*), night fighters; *Zerstoerer-* (*ZG*), twin-engined fighters; *Kampf-* (*KG*), bombers; *Stuka-* (*StG*), dive bombers; *Schlacht-* (*SG*), ground attack; and *Transportgeschwader* (*TG*), transports. Quite different were the units of the so-called *Lehrgeschwader* (*LG*), formed to test new aircraft of all types under operational conditions and to try out new tactics.

Reconnaissance units were usually independent *Gruppen*, *Aufklaerungsgruppen* (*Aufkl.Gr*). Other independent *Gruppen* were formed from time to time for specific tasks, for example *Kampfgruppe 100* (*KGr 100*), a specialist pathfinder unit.

All *Geschwader* and independent *Gruppen* were numbered with arabic numerals, for example *Kampfgeschwader 55*, *Jagdgruppe 106* or *Aufklarungsgruppe 124*.

Usually, however, a *Gruppe* formed part of a *Geschwader* and was numbered in Roman numerals before the *Geschwader* designation; thus the Fourth *Gruppe* of *KG 51* was written as *IV./KG 51* (a dot placed behind a numeral in German has the same meaning as 'th' in English). Similarly, the *Stab* (headquarters) flight of *Stukageschwader 3* would be abbreviated as *Stab/StG 3*.

The *Staffeln* within a *Geschwader* were numbered consecutively, using Arabic numerals. Thus in a simple unit comprising three *Gruppen* each of three *Staffeln*, the 1st, 2nd and 3rd *Staffeln* comprised the *I. Gruppe*, the 4th, 5th and 6th *Staffeln* comprised the *II. Gruppe*, and the 7th, 8th and 9th *Staffeln* comprised the *III. Gruppe*. The third *Staffel* of *Kampfgeschwader 53* was therefore abbreviated to *3./KG 53*, and was part of *I./KG 53*.

3
The Fighter Force

Fighter-versus-Fighter Tactics

The *Luftwaffe* tactics for fighter-versus-fighter combat were characterised by aggressive use of forces, combined with the exploitation of known performance advantages over enemy fighters. The basic fighting unit was the *Rotte* (cell) or pair, comprising a leader (*Rottefuehrer*) and wing-man (*Katchmarek*). During cruising flight the two aircraft flew almost in line abreast about 200 yards apart, each pilot concentrating his search inwards so that he covered his partner's blind areas. In combat it was the wing-man's duty to guard his leader's tail, while the latter did the fighting.

Two *Rotten* made up a *Schwarm* or Flight, with the leading *Rotte* flying to one side and slightly ahead of the other; some German fighter leaders, however, prefered to fly with the aircraft of their *Schwarm* in line abreast. A *Staffel* formation comprised three *Schwaerme* stepped up in line astern.

While operating in areas where contact with the enemy was likely, fighters maintained a high cruising speed. At such a time it was obviously undesirable to reduce speed during turns; but if the 600-yard wide *Schwarm* formation was held and turned through a wide angle, the aircraft on the outside of the turn inevitably became stragglers. To overcome this problem the 'cross-over turn' was evolved, in which each pilot held his speed and simply changed his position in the formation during the manoeuvre (see diagram).

During the early part of the Second World War the Messerschmitt 109 had a superior altitude performance to the Polish, French and British fighters which opposed it. In general, therefore, the German tactics were to get above their opponents and attempt to 'bounce' them, if possible from out of the sun; after a single firing pass, the German fighters would use the speed they had gained in their dive to climb back into position for repeat attacks. Since their opponents almost always flew slower fighters with greater manoeuvrability, the Germans preferred to avoid turning fights.

If they were themselves 'bounced' the German fighter pilots' normal reply was to turn individually to meet the attack. If there was no time for this the German fighters would often bunt over into a dive, which exploited the direct

injection fuel system fitted to their Daimler Benz or BMW engines (if this manoeuvre was imitated by aircraft with normal float carburetters, their engines
were likely to cut due to fuel starvation). An alternative escape manoeuvre was
the *Abschwung* (American 'Split-S'), a half roll pulled through into a steep dive
at full throttle; when used to get away from an enemy this method resulted in a
considerable loss of height – between 10,000 and 15,000 feet – which precluded
its use except in desperate situations. Whichever escape manoeuvre was
employed, it was usual to combine it with a turn in the direction of the attack,
to increase the problems of deflection shooting.

   Generally these tactics, which allowed formation and *Rotte* commanders
considerable room for initiative, served the German fighter force well. During
the Battle of Britain, however, the German fighters were ordered to remain
close to the bombers they escorted; on no account were they to engage
the enemy unless they or their bombers were directly threatened. Since the
bombers cruised somewhat more slowly than the fighters, the latter had to
weave to maintain station if they were also to keep up a high cruising speed in
the danger area. These instructions nullified the effectiveness of the otherwise
superior German fighter tactics, and resulted in the surrender of the initiative
in combat to the RAF. In other theatres of action the *Luftwaffe*, like the Allied
fighter forces later in the war, found it more effective if only a small proportion
of the fighters stayed close to the bombers while the remainder ranged
aggressively ahead and swept the area clear of enemy fighters.

Fighter-versus-Bomber Tactics

Up to the autumn of 1942 the standard German tactics against bombers
operating by day involved stern or quarter attacks, by *Rotten* or *Schwaerme*.
When they came against the formations of American heavy bombers, however,
with their defensive batteries of heavy machine guns, the German fighters
began to suffer disconcerting losses.

   The first major variation in tactics was to attack from head-on, thus en-
abling the fighters to strike at the American B-17 and B-24 bombers in a position where the latters' defensive armaments were less powerful and also where
their armour protection was less effective. During such attacks the usual
method was to make contact with the American formation and trail it for a
short time while the German fighter leader gauged its course. That done the
fighters would overtake the bombers, flying just beyond the range of their
defensive fire; when they were about two miles ahead, the fighters would turn
through a half circle and go into their firing runs. The American bombers
cruised at about 175mph and the German fighters attacked at about 300mph,
so the closing speed between the two was nearly 500mph. This allowed the
fighter pilots time for only a brief firing pass: opening fire at 500 yards and
breaking off at 100 yards gave them less than two seconds. To bring down
heavy bombers during such an attack called for exceptionally good shooting,
and the problem of range estimation proved to be beyond all but the best of
pilots. On the other hand there was a good chance that during a *Staffel* attack
one or two bombers might be damaged sufficiently to force them to leave the
protection of their formation; these could then be finished off.

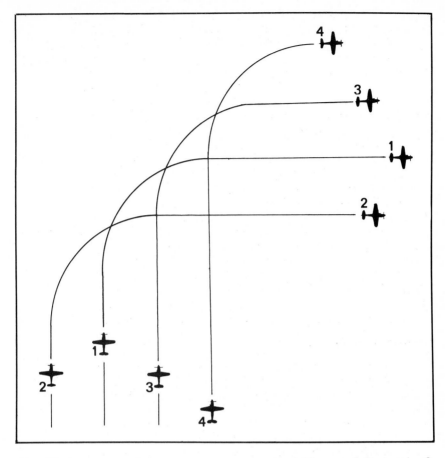

Above: The 'cross-over turn'.

Below: The Messerschmitt 109 was the most-used German fighter type during the Second World War and more than thirty thousand were produced. The example illustrated, a G model, carries the Ace-of-Spades badge of *Jagdgeschwader 53* on the nose; the vertical bar on the rear fuselage indicates that it belonged to the *III. Gruppe./via Schliephake*

During the spring and summer of 1943 the *Luftwaffe* tried air-to-air bombing and rocket attacks, from outside the range of the bombers' defensive fire, in an attempt to split up the American formations before the cannon-armed fighters went in to attack. In both cases these weapons proved inaccurate, however, and although there were some spectacular successes they were few and far between.

The combination of head-on, quarter and rear attacks continued in use from the close of 1942 until the spring of 1944; then, due to the increasing strength and aggressiveness of the American escort fighters, German fighter formations even in *Gruppe* strength found it difficult to get through to the bombers. The new situation placed the German planners on the horns of a dilemma: if their fighters were to achieve any degree of success against the rugged American bombers they needed to carry heavy batteries of cannon and rockets; but if they did, they were easy meat for the more nimble American escort fighters. To overcome this problem Generalmajor Galland introduced separate 'heavy' *Sturmgruppen* to engage the bombers while covering 'light' fighter *Gruppen* held off the escorts. One *Sturmgruppe* and two covering *Gruppen* comprised a *Gefechtsverband* (battle formation) with a strength of more than a hundred aircraft. During the summer and autumn of 1944 the *Gefechtsverbaende* showed that they could cause great slaughter if they were able to get into position behind a 'box' of American bombers. On the other hand the huge German formations took a long time to form up and were unwieldy during their approach flights; frequently the wide-ranging American escorts were able to find them and break them up before they could get anywhere near the bombers.

During the final nine months of the war the Luftwaffe employed its slowly expanding force of jet and rocket fighters against the American bomber formations, but never in sufficient numbers to achieve any great success. The speed of these aircraft was so great that they did not require top cover to get through the escorts, but as they closed on the slow-flying bombers this very speed could become an embarrassment since it resulted in a very short firing pass. To overcome this problem the German jet fighter pilots evolved special tactics. They would dive through the escorts at speeds of about 550mph, aiming for a position about one mile behind and 1,500 feet beneath their quarry; when they reached this position the pilots made a high-G pull-up to 'dump' speed, then levelled off. At the end of this manoeuvre the jet fighters were in an ideal position to attack: they were inside the escorting fighter screen, about 1,000 yards behind and on the same level as the bombers chosen as targets, and with an overtaking speed of about 100mph. If the fighter carried rockets it would fire these first, then follow up with cannon fire. During these attacks each jet fighter concentrated on a single bomber; there was insufficient time during the firing pass for more than one aircraft to be engaged. When about 100 yards from the bomber the jet fighter pilot would pull up and break away overhead it, to avoid any falling debris.

Night Fighter Tactics

From the beginning of the war until May 1940 the night air defence of the

Top: At the beginning of the war the
Messerschmitt 110 was the best twin-engined
fighter in service in any air force; it was to
prove particularly useful in the bomber-
destroyer and fighter-bomber roles. This
example, an E sub-type fitted with bomb
racks under the wings and fuselage, belonged
to 7. *Staffel* of *Zerstoerergeschwader 1./Radinger*

Above: A Focke Wulf 190 A-8/R8 of *11.
(Sturmgruppe) J.G. 300,* photographed at
Loebnitz late in 1944. This sub-type carried
considerable armour protection for the pilot
and was fitted with a bomber-destroying
armament of two 3-cm cannon just outboard
of the main undercarriage legs./*Schroeder*

Messerschmitt 410 bomber-destroyer, bearing the Wasp insignia of *Zerstoerergeschwader 1*. This aircraft carried two 2-cm cannon in the lower part of the nose and two more in the under-fuselage tray, four machine guns across the centre of the nose and four wing-mounted 21-cm rocket launchers./*via Redemann*

Top: A Messerschmitt 262 jet fighter of *Jagdgeschwader* 7 seen being readied for take-off in the spring of 1945./*via Schliephake*

Above: Me 262 at Lechfeld base south of Augsburg./*via Schliephake*

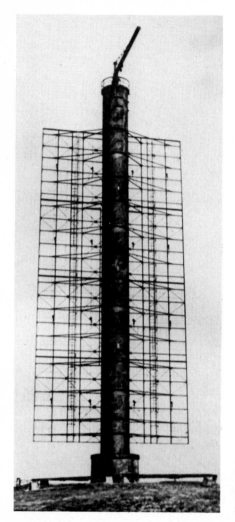

Above: The best German long-range early-warning radar was the *Wassermann*; this example, an S model, was situated at radar station *Viper* in north-western Denmark. The radar operated on spot frequencies in the band 120 to 145 megacycles and had a maximum range of 190 miles against high-flying aircraft. The aerials were mounted on a cylindrical steel tower 198 feet high; an interesting feature of this equipment was the method of electronically sweeping the beam in the vertical plane, to provide a height finding facility./*Ewald via Heise*

Above: The *Freya* was the most-used German surveillance radar; this example operated near Leipzig. This equipment appeared in many forms during the war and by the end of the conflict it operated on frequencies between 50 and 190 megacycles and had a maximum range of about 100 miles against high-flying aircraft; most *Freya* sets had no height-finding capability. The additional aerial at the top of the main frame, on the set in the photograph, belonged to the identification equipment./*via Heise*

German homeland was almost entirely the responsibility of the *Flak* arm of the *Luftwaffe*. The small and ineffectual night fighter force comprised a few single-engined machines, for the most part Messerschmitt 109s, flown by pilots who had specialised in the role. They relied on searchlights in the target area to illuminate their targets for them; the tactics bore the code-name *Helle Nachtjagd* (illuminated night fighting). Owing to the small number of night fighters, however, and the few RAF bombers operating over Germany (for the most part leaflet raiders), there were few 'kills' during this phase.

In May 1940 the RAF opened its bombing offensive against German industrial targets, and the ineffectiveness of the *Flak* defences in preventing attacks led to a massive expansion and re-organisation of the night fighter arm. By the middle of 1941 the night fighter arm had evolved into a powerful force with some 250 twin-engined fighters, Messerschmitt 110s, Junkers 88s and Dornier 17s, backed by an increasingly effective ground control and reporting organisation.

One of the drawbacks of the *Helle Nachtjagd* tactics was that, since the searchlights were concentrated round the more important towns and cities, these methods could achieve little outside the actual target zone. And, orbiting over these defended areas, the night fighters had often been illuminated and engaged by 'friendly' anti-aircraft gunners. To overcome this problem of identification Generalmajor Kammhuber, the architect of the new night fighter organisation, repositioned the night fighter engagement area clear of the German cities – and therefore clear of the gun-defended areas. Along the line from Schleswig Holstein to Liège, which lay astride the route used by RAF bombers attacking Germany, he set up ground control radar stations at twenty-mile intervals. Each of these ground stations was equipped with a *Freya* radar for area surveillance and two *Wuerzburg* precision radars; one *Wuerzburg* was used to track an individual bomber while the other tracked the night fighter. Using information from the two precision radars plotted out on a special table, a fighter control officer on the ground directed the night fighter into position within visual range behind the target. These new tactics bore the code-name *Himmelbett* (four-poster bed).

In addition to the units engaged in the purely defensive *Himmelbett* tactics, Kammhuber controlled a *Gruppe*, I./*NJG 2*, whose Ju 88s and Do 17s engaged in offensive intruder (*Fernnachtjagd*) operations over the British Isles. These aircraft would patrol overhead airfields thought likely to be active when bombing attacks were being mounted, and bomb and strafe whenever activity was seen on the ground. These intruder sorties caused a great deal of disruption; but in the autumn of 1941 the shortage of night fighter units to operate with the expanding number of *Himmelbett* ground stations, coupled with the general over-extension of the *Luftwaffe* as the Russian campaign got into its stride, lead to their cessation. I./*NJG 2* was re-deployed to the defensive role, and after that there was no *Luftwaffe* unit regularly and exclusively engaged in night intruder operations over British airfields.

Between the summer of 1941 and the summer of 1942 the line of *Himmelbett* stations gradually extended, until it ran from the northern tip of Denmark to the Swiss frontier; this defensive barrier was shaped like an inverted sickle, its

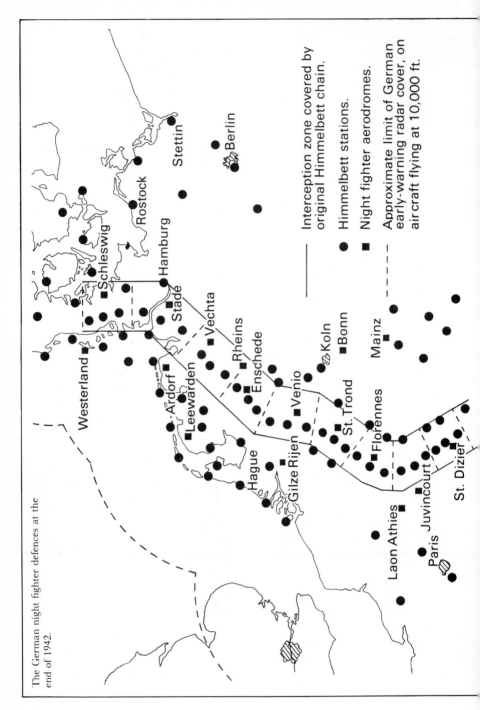

The German night fighter defences at the end of 1942.

Interception zone covered by original Himmelbett chain.

Himmelbett stations.

Night fighter aerodromes.

Approximate limit of German early-warning radar cover, on aircraft flying at 10,000 ft.

Berlin

Stettin

Rostock

Schleswig

Hamburg

Stade

Vechta

Rheins

Enschede

Koln

Bonn

Mainz

Westerland

Ardorf

Leewarden

Venlo

St. Trond

Florennes

Hague

Gilze Rijen

St. Dizier

Laon Athies

Juvincourt

Paris

'handle' running through Denmark from north to south, its 'blade' curving through northern Germany, Holland, Belgium and eastern France. In the late spring of 1942 RAF Bomber Command began employing concentrated 'stream' tactics to saturate the *Himmelbett* stations along the bombers' route; Kammhuber responded by erecting additional ground stations in front of and behind his line, to extend its width and thus increase the number of bombers that could be engaged during any one attack.

From the beginning of 1942 two important new radar devices began to enter service in quantity, improving the efficiency of the *Luftwaffe*: the *Wuerzburg Reise* (Giant *Wuerzburg*) ground fighter control set, which replaced the small *Wuerzburg* at the *Himmelbett* stations; and the *Lichtenstein BC* lightweight radar, which was gradually fitted into all fighters employed on night operations.

The *Himmelbett* tactics took a steady toll of the RAF night bombers until July 1943, when Bomber Command introduced its potent countermeasure: 'Window'. 'Window' was the RAF code-name for thin strips of aluminium foil, initially measuring 30cms by 1.5cms, which were dropped in bundles of a thousand at a time at one-minute intervals from each of the bombers in the stream. These bundles blossomed into fluttering clouds of radar-reflective strips which saturated the screens of the *Wuerzburg*, *Wuerzburg Reise* and *Lichtenstein* radars with scores of false targets. At a stroke, the *Himmelbett* system of close-controlled night fighting was set to nought.

The German reply to the British use of 'Window' was a sweeping re-organisation of its night fighter tactics. Two methods of operation emerged, *Wilde Sau* (Wild Boar) and *Zahme Sau* (Tame Boar). The *Wilde Sau* tactics called for the concentration of the night fighter units over the target itself, where the massed searchlights and the Pathfinders' marker flares lit up the sky and silhouetted the bombers for the fighters. Thus the latter could now attack without using radar; this meant that the 'Window' jamming had no effect on the system. The tactics bore a strong resemblance to the earlier *Helle Nachtjagd* methods; to solve the previous problem of aircraft identification the anti-aircraft gunners were ordered to fuse their shells to explode at or below designated levels, above which the fighters operated. A special *Geschwader*, *JG300*, was set up to operate single-seat Messerschmitt 109 and Focke Wulf 190 fighters in the *Wilde Sau* role.

The radar-equipped twin-engined night fighters could also join in the *Wilde Sau* battles at the target. But to use their potential to the full they employed their own *Zahme Sau* tactics; under this system the Fighter Divisional head-quarters on the ground broadcast orders to the fighters operating in their areas, to direct them to those points where the 'Window' concentrations were the greatest; once there, the night fighter crews were to search for their quarry visually. In this way scores of night fighters could be controlled and brought into action with the bombers; the intention was to set up long-running battles with the raiding forces for as long as contact could be maintained.

To strengthen the *Zahme Sau* tactics, three new airborne electronic devices entered service during the latter part of 1943: *Lichtenstein SN-2*, *Naxos* and *Flensburg*. The *Lichtenstein SN-2* was a completely new radar set for night fighters, to replace the earlier *Lichtenstein BC;* the *SN-2* worked on frequencies which were

Above: Until it was neutralised by the 'Window' metal foil dropped from the RAF bombers, in the summer of 1943, the *Wuerzburg Reise* was the most important German medium range precision radar. Developed from the smaller *Wuerzburg*, it was fitted with a parabolic reflector 7.5 metres (nearly 25 feet) in diameter which gave it a maximum pick-up range of about 50 miles, and it had a tracking accuracy of ± 50 yards in range and ±¼ degree in bearing. Initially it worked on spot frequencies around 560 megacycles; later, modifications enabled it to work in the band 450 to 600 megacycles./*via Heise*

Below: For the middle four years of the war the Messerschmitt 110 equipped the majority of the German night fighter units. The example depicted, a G model, carries the aerials for the SN-2 radar which operated on spot frequencies between 73 and 91 megacycles and which had a maximum range of about 4 miles./*RC Seeley*

not jammed by the type of 'Window' then being used by the RAF. *Naxos* and *Flensburg* were both radar homing devices, the former on the emissions of the British H2S blind bombing and navigational radar, and the latter on the emissions from the British 'Monica' tail-warning radar.

We shall now examine a typical *Zahme Sau* operation, to observe the way these tactics were being used during the early part of 1944. While at readiness the night fighter crews would relax in dimly-lit huts close to their aircraft dispersals, kept informed of the progress of the enemy bombers by broadcast announcements. Usually there was sufficient warning of the approach of the raiders for the German crews to walk out to their aircraft and strap in without undue haste. As the night fighters taxied out to the take-off point their crews tuned in to their fighter broadcast frequency and received the latest information on the position, probable strength, course and probable target of the bombers, and also the code-name of the radio beacon they were to make for after take-off.

Once airborne, the night fighters would climb to the bombers' altitude (usually around 20,000 feet) and make for their assembly beacon; while they waited for the air situation to clarify to the fighter controllers on the ground, as many as fifty night fighters might be orbiting in the darkness round a single beacon – a flight safety hazard which would be unthinkable in peace time, though in the event there were remarkably few collisions.

As the bomber stream penetrated deeper into German-occupied territory and its intentions became clearer to those on the ground directing the defensive night fighters, the controllers broadcast orders to these fighters to move from beacon to beacon towards the raiders; finally, they were ordered to leave a designated beacon on a set heading and seek out the bombers. Sometimes the night fighter crews would make contact by picking up the bombers' emissions on their *Naxos* or *Flensburg* receivers; sometimes they would first see the aircraft on their *SN-2* radar; and on other occasions the first indication of the presence of the enemy would be the judder of their fighter as it passed through the turbulent wake left by the heavy bombers.

Once they were in contact with the bomber stream, the German night fighter crews had strict orders that they were not to attack before they had passed back to the Divisional control centre the location of the bombers and their heading; this information could then be re-broadcast to bring other night fighters into action.

The usual German night fighter tactics were to try to approach the bomber selected as target from slightly below; in that way they themselves were difficult to see against the dark background of the earth, whilst the bomber was silhouetted against the light background of the sky. If the night fighter was seen during its approach the bomber would usually go into a corkscrew evasive manoeuvre, and the fighter pilot had to make the best attack he could under the circumstances; if a violent corkscrew was flown by a skilful bomber pilot, even the best German night fighter pilots had difficulty in hitting the target and the bomber usually escaped. If, on the other hand, the bomber crew had been less vigilant and the night fighter was able to get into position in the blind area underneath them without being seen, their chances of escape were slim.

Attacks from underneath could be made with the upward-firing cannon (code-named *Schraege Musik*), or the night fighter pilot could pull up his nose so that his forward-firing cannon raked the bomber as it flew past. The usual aiming point was the wing, close to one of the engines, for there lay the inflammable fuel tanks; since the night fighters attacked from short ranges – often within 75 yards – it was considered unwise to aim at the fuselage and thus risk detonating the bomb load, for the fighter might itself be destroyed in the resultant explosion.

The *Zahme Sau* tactics reached their zenith of effectiveness when, on the night of March 30th/31st 1944, night fighters employing these methods brought down the majority of the 107 heavy bombers destroyed by the German defences. This success of the twin-engined night fighters led to the single-seat *Wilde Sau* being transfered to the daylight air defence role, for operations against the American bombers.

From the late spring of 1944 until the end of the war the German night fighter force continued to employ *Zahme Sau* as its main tactical method. This period was, however, one of unremitting decline for the force: the increasing weight and effectiveness of the RAF radar jamming, the fuel shortage and the resultant end to training, the increasing degree of Allied air superiority over Germany by day and by night and, finally, the advance of the Allied ground forces, all combined to bring about a collapse of the night defences.

During the final year of the war the Junkers 88G transcended the Messerschmitt 110 in importance in the night fighter force. This example, carrying the 7J code of *Nachtjagdgeschwader 102*, was fitted with two 2 cm cannon in an upward-firing *Schraege Musik* installation. The bulge on the top of the cockpit canopy housed the aerial for the *Naxos* homing device.

4
The Bomber Force

Horizontal Bombing Tactics

The tactics employed by aircraft making horizontal bombing attacks were governed almost entirely by the strength of the defences likely to be met and the nature of the target. To bomb with the *Lotfe* tachometric sight, the standard type fitted to German bombers for most of the war, a straight-and-level bombing run of about 40 seconds was required. Alternatively the crew could attack from low level, in which case the pilot released the bombs 'by eye'.

Against the easiest targets, those lacking any form of defence, bombers could make accurate attacks from medium level; crews would attack individually, making two or even three deliberate bombing runs and releasing only when the bomb aimer was satisfied that he would hit the target. For the *Luftwaffe* the opportunities to carry out such attacks were rare, however, and they became rarer still as the war progressed.

The effect of anti-aircraft defences round a target was to force the bombers to attack from greater altitudes, where they were less vulnerable; but this safety was bought only at the expense of bombing accuracy. To prevent the enemy gunners from concentrating all their fire on individual bombers, the raiders would attack in loose formations.

If enemy fighter attacks were also expected, the German bombers would fly in mututally-protecting formations. If it was engaged by anti-aircraft guns the formation would open out, if it was attacked by fighters it would close up. Escorting fighters almost invariably cruised faster than the bombers they were to protect, so those assigned to close escort duties flew a weaving path to maintain station on their charges. During raids escorted by single-engined fighters, the latters' short endurance usually dictated that the bombers had to take the most direct route from the fighter rendezvous point to the target; whenever possible, the rendezvous point was chosen so that the straight line from it to the target did not pass over heavily-defended areas.

At the target the bomber crews aimed their bombs individually, unless they had previously been briefed to pattern-bomb; in the latter case the formation and bomb stick spacing were tailored to the size of the target, and all aircraft

The largest type of conventional bomb employed operationally by the *Luftwaffe* was the SC 2500 Max. It was 12 feet 9 inches long and 2 feet 8 inches in diameter and was too large to fit into the bomb bay of any German bomber; the example depicted was about to be loaded on to the external rack of a Heinkel 111 of *I./KG 100./Baetcher*

released on the radioed signal from the formation leader. If special types of bombs were used, these sometimes dictated the bombing altitude; for example, armour piercing bombs had to be released from high level, or they would not reach a high enough velocity to punch their way into the target before exploding.

When enemy gun and fighter defences were too strong to allow daylight attacks to be made without risking unacceptable losses, the German bombers resorted to night attacks; this greatly reduced the accuracy of the bombing, however. During its night attacks on Britain from the summer of 1941 until the late spring of 1941 the *Luftwaffe* employed the so-called 'Crocodile' tactics; aircraft of the same *Gruppe* or *Geschwader* flew down the same route at about four-minute (twelve-mile) intervals. Allowing for a dispersion of about seven miles to either side of the path, and 10,000 feet in altitude (the aircraft flew at between 10,000 and 20,000 feet), this meant an average of one bomber per *330 cubic miles* of airspace. Units were ordered to attack at widely-spaced intervals, to cause disruption at the target for as long as possible; sometimes the night raids were spread over as long as ten hours, from just after dusk until just before dawn.

At the outbreak of the Second World War the *Luftwaffe*, alone amongst the world's air forces, possessed radio aids to assist its bomber crews to find their targets at night or in bad weather. The simplest of the systems was code-named *Knickebein* (bent leg); it used two radio beams, one to delineate the track to the target and the second to cross the first at the bomb release point. The beam signals were picked up by the same receiver that picked up the German airfield-approach beam signals, so no special equipment was required in the bombers. Using *Knickebein* transmitters situated along the coast of Holland and northern France, the bombers were able to navigate with reasonable accuracy over central and southern England. However, in electronic warfare it is an accepted axiom that systems that are simple and cheap to operate are usually simple and cheap to counter; and so it proved with *Knickebein*. Within two months of its discovery, the RAF had formed and deployed its own counter-measures organisation which successfully neutralised *Knickebein*.

In addition to *Knickebein*, the *Luftwaffe* employed two separate precision target-finding systems for its pathfinder *Gruppen*: the *X-Geraet* used by *Kampfgruppe 100*, and the *Y-Geraet* used by the *III.Gruppe* of *KG 26*. These were more complex than the earlier system, and both required that special equipment be carried by the aircraft which used them. Initially the *X* and *Y* systems had some success in guiding the pathfinders to their targets, which they marked using incendiary bombs (the *X* device was responsible for the accurate marking which preceded the devastating attack on Coventry in November 1940). Soon the RAF learnt of their working, however, and again the jamming proved effective.

After the summer of 1941 the *Luftwaffe* bomber force conducted only spasmodic attacks on Britain, with peaks of activity during the 'Baedeker' raids in the spring and early summer of 1942, and the *Steinbock* attacks early in 1944. During these night actions the *Luftwaffe* abandoned its earlier 'Crocodile' tactics, for these would have presented the greatly improved gun and fighter defences with an almost ideal succession of individual targets. Instead the Germans adopted

Top: At the outbreak of the Second World War the Heinkel 111 equipped about three-quarters of the twin-engined bomber units in the *Luftwaffe*. In this photograph, taken in the summer of 1943, the examples depicted were of the H model and belonged to *I./KG 100*; the yellow band on the rear fuselage indicated that these aircraft were operational on the Russian front./*Baetcher*

Above: During the course of the Second World War the Junkers 88 became the mainstay of the German medium bomber force. In addition to its initial roles of horizontal- and dive-bomber, this aircraft also served successfully as minelayer, torpedo bomber, ground attack aircraft, pathfinder, reconnaissance aircraft and night fighter. The example depicted was an A-4 bomber and belonged to *II./KG 54*; the white band on the rear fuselage indicated that it was operational in the Mediterranean area. Two SC-250 bombs can be seen, on the external racks between the engines and the fuselage./*via Schiephake*

Top: An Arado 234B jet bomber of *Kampfgeschwader 76* getting airborne assisted by a pair of 1,100 pound rocket booster pods; when the pods had exhausted their fuel, they were jettisoned. The aircraft's bomb load, mounted externally under the engine nacelles, is just visible./*KG 76 Archiv*

Above: Although it has the external appearance of a twin-engined aircraft, the Heinkel 177 was in fact powered by four engines with two coupled to each propeller. Intended to equip a large part of the German bomber force, the He 177 proved unreliable in service and only six *Gruppen* were fully operational with the type. The example depicted was an A-3 model belonging to *I./KG 100* and was photographed at the time of the *Steinbock* attacks on Britain early in 1944./*RC Seeley*

bomber 'stream' tactics similar to those employed by RAF Bomber Command, sending the raiding force in a mass along the same route for a concentrated attack lasting some twenty minutes; in this way the defences were presented with far more targets than they could possibly engage during the short time of passage of the enemy aircraft. During many of these later attacks on Britain a modified type of *Y-Geraet* was used to assist the pathfinders to find and mark the targets; this made use of several different frequency channels and was switched on only at the last moment, to make jamming more difficult.

We shall now examine one of the *Steinbock* attacks, that on London on the night of April 18th 1944, to see the German tactics at the peak of their development. The force of about 125 bombers, Ju 88s and Ju 188s, He 177s, Do 217s and Me 410s, funneled together over the radio beacon at Noordwijk in Holland, then streamed across the North Sea in a climb towards East Anglia. On the way they passed over an on-track fixing point, comprising six flame floats laid in the sea by pathfinder aircraft. The bombers crossed the English coast just to the north of Orfordness at altitudes above 17,000 feet; twice per minute, each aircraft released a bundle of *Dueppel* radar reflective foil to confuse the defences. The raiders continued westwards to their next turning point to the east of Newmarket, which the pathfinders had marked with red parachute flares. The attacking force then turned on a south-westerly heading towards London. As they entered the target area the bombers began a slow descent and released *Dueppel* as fast as possible, to make predicted anti-aircraft fire more difficult. The raiders levelled out for their bombing runs, aiming at the clusters of red parachute flares laid out by the pathfinders. Once their bombs were gone the attackers resumed their descent and turned south-eastwards on to their withdrawal heading. During their dash for the coast some of the bombers reached speeds of more than 400mph; this, in combination with the descent of about 600 feet per minute and the *Dueppel*, gave the defending ground gunners and night fighter crews a difficult engagement problem. That night British night fighters claimed nine of the bombers shot down, but the majority of these were hit while en route to the target.

The final part of the *Luftwaffe* bomber offensive against Britain lasted from the summer of 1944 until the early part of 1945. During this phase specially modified Heinkel 111s aimed Fi 103 flying bombs at London and other targets in Britain, from launching points off the east coast. To avoid the defences the bombers made their approach flights at night and at low level; when in range they would pop up to 1,500 feet, accelerate to about 200mph to give the Fi 103 flying speed and loose off the missile, then quickly get back to low altitude for their escape. As a method of bombardment the air-launched flying bomb was grossly inaccurate, however. The fifty-per cent zone* for weapons launched in this way was of the order of 24 miles; thus, even without the defences, there was only a *one-in-thirty-two* chance of such a bomb hitting the sprawling 12-mile-diameter circle of the Greater London built-up area.

---

* The 'fifty-per cent zone', or fifty per cent circular error, is the radius of the circle, centred on the target, in which the best fifty per cent of a number of individually-aimed bombs or missiles falls using a stated weapons system. It is the standard method of comparing one method of aiming with another.

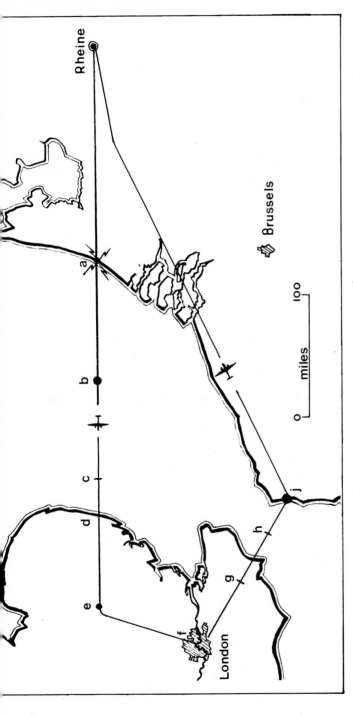

Map showing the route flown by the bombers of I./KG 100 during the attack on London on April 18th, 1944. A – radio beacon at Noordwijk, over which the German bomber force assembled. B – fixing point comprising six flame floats, laid in the sea by pathfinder aircraft. C – position at which the aircraft began to release *Dueppel* foil to jam the British radar. D – Coast-in just to the north of Orfordness, at altitudes around 17,000 feet. E – Route turning point east of Newmarket, marked by red parachute flares dropped by pathfinders. F – bombers commenced descent shortly before target and began releasing *Dueppel* at maximum rate; bombing altitude about 16,500 feet. G – during the withdrawal flight the bombers descended at about 600 feet per minute, making a high-speed dash for the coast. H – cease dropping *Dueppel*. J – altitude crossing the French coast, 2,500 feet.

37

Top: The Junkers 87 was the tactical dive-bomber most used by the *Luftwaffe* during the Second World War. The aircraft seen here were D models belonging to *Sturzkampfgeschwader 77./via Schliephake*

Above: There are several points of interest on this photograph of a Ju 87D of *II./StG 77,* taken on the occasion of the successful completion of 300 operational missions by an unidentified member of the unit. The two SC-50 bombs on the rack nearest the camera had each been fitted with a *Dinort* extension rod, to detonate them just above the ground; under the wing may be seen the dive brake in the retracted position; the wheel spats have been removed, as was often the case during operations from muddy airfields; at the top of the undercarriage leg can be seen the propeller for the wind-driven 'Screamer'./*via Schliephake*

Finally, mention must be made of the tactics used by the jet-propelled Arado 234, the most advanced horizontal bomber to enter service in the *Luftwaffe* and the only such aircraft at the close of the war to have the speed to outrun the opposing interceptors by day. During high level attacks the pilot of this single-seater had a heavy work load, since alone he had to perform all of the tasks involved in the bombing run; to assist him the aircraft carried an advanced three-axis auto-pilot, which was linked to the *Lotfe* bombsight. After the pilot had flown to a previously-planned initial point short of the target, he engaged the autopilot. Then he *disconnected* the normal control column and swung it out of his way to the right, loosened his seat straps and leant forward to the bomb-aiming position. Crouching over the eyepiece of the *Lotfe* sight, the pilot adjusted its controls to hold the target in the centre of the graticule; these adjustments were fed into the bombsight computer, which in turn fed correction demands into the autopilot to position the bomber on the correct flight path for the bombing run. When the sight computer calculated that the aircraft was at the bomb release point, it automatically released the bombs. It remained only for the pilot to regain his seat and tighten his straps, re-connect his control column, disengage the automatic pilot and turn for home. During the closing months of the war the Arado 234s of *KG 76* carried out several such attacks from altitudes of about 30,000 feet; they found that the greatest handicap was cloud cover at the target, which frequently prevented visual bombing from such a height.

The tactical methods described in this section were those most frequently used by the *Luftwaffe* medium and heavy bomber force. The list given is by no means complete, however, for unit commanders often tailored their tactics to counter the defences met in specific areas or to meet the needs of specific targets.

Dive Bombing Tactics

In this section the tactics employed with the Junkers 87 are described in detail; the dive-bombing methods used by the twin-engined Junkers 88 were essentially similar, though the actual dive was somewhat shallower (60 degrees during the early part of the war, reduced to 50 degrees later).

The steep-dive attack was one of the most accurate ways of bombing. On the completion of their course at the specialist Dive Bomber School, crews were expected to be able to get fifty per cent of their bombs within 25 metres (27 yards) of the centre of the target; the comparable distances for high-flying horizontal bombers were two or three times larger. Furthermore, against operational targets, which were usually defended by anti-aircraft guns, the errors for all types of bombing were two or even three times as great as those indicated on the training ranges. Thus, although the dive-bombing attack was not accurate enough to be worth-while against small, hard targets such as individual tanks, it was very effective against soft targets, such as motor vehicles, which were vulnerable to near misses. Against (say) a circular fortification with a radius of 80 yards, with moderately heavy gun defences, a *Staffel* of Ju 87s stood a good chance of scoring four or five hits with large bombs.

In each case the nature of the target dictated the bomb load carried by the

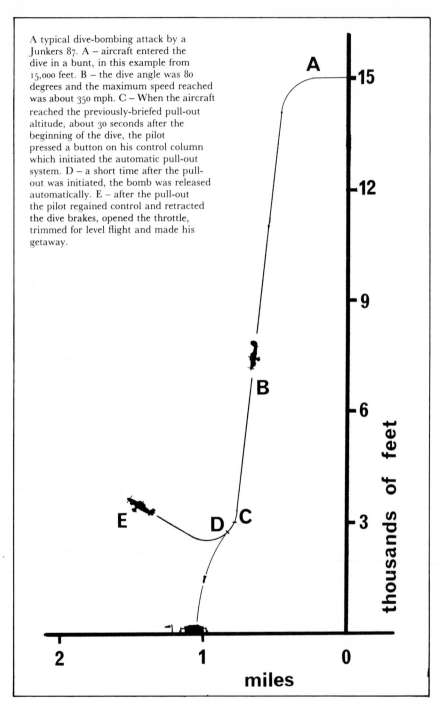

A typical dive-bombing attack by a Junkers 87. A – aircraft entered the dive in a bunt, in this example from 15,000 feet. B – the dive angle was 80 degrees and the maximum speed reached was about 350 mph. C – When the aircraft reached the previously-briefed pull-out altitude, about 30 seconds after the beginning of the dive, the pilot pressed a button on his control column which initiated the automatic pull-out system. D – a short time after the pull-out was initiated, the bomb was released automatically. E – after the pull-out the pilot regained control and retracted the dive brakes, opened the throttle, trimmed for level flight and made his getaway.

Ju 87; against a concreted fortification, for example, a single SD-500 would be used; against field artillery positions, a typical load would be one SC-250 under the fuselage and four SC-50s under the wings.*

When approaching their target the Ju 87s would, typically, fly in three-aircraft Vics (*Ketten*) at about 15,000 feet, cruising at 150mph. Larger formations would be made up of several of these Vics in line astern, with a spacing of about 300 yards between aircraft, up to a usual maximum of about thirty machines (*Gruppe* strength). If there were fighters flying close escort, these would follow a weaving path behind and slightly above the dive-bombers; as the force neared the target the escort would split, one-third remaining at height while the remainder descended to about 3,000 feet to be in position to protect the bombers from enemy fighters as they pulled out of their dives.

Prior to entering his dive the Ju 87 pilot switched on his reflector sight, trimmed the aircraft for the dive, set the pull-out altitude on the contact altimeter, closed the radiator flaps, throttled back the engine and opened the ventilation air supply to the windscreen (to prevent possible misting as the aircraft entered the moist air lower down). Finally he switched on the wind-driven 'Screamer' (if required) and opened the dive brakes; the hydraulic operation of the brakes automatically lowered an elevator tab, to counter the severe nose-up trim-change which would otherwise result.

The signal to attack was given by the formation leader starting his dive. For strikes on smaller targets the aircraft would move into echelon during the approach, and peel off and attack in line astern. Against larger targets (for example, harbours or marshalling yards), the dive-bombers would bunt over and attack by Vics; the pilot was able to see directly beneath his aircraft through a small window set in the floor, and so was able to judge when to begin his bunt.

Once it was established in its dive, typically at an angle of 80 degrees, the Ju 87 with extended dive-brakes gained speed only gradually. It took about 8,000 feet for it to reach its limiting speed of about 350 mph, after which its velocity remained constant. The accuracy of the attack depended upon the accuracy with which the selected dive angle was maintained. To assist him the pilot had etched lines on the side panels of his canopy, rather like a protractor, on which he could align the horizon and read off his angle; after some practice, however, pilots were able to judge their dive angle to within fine limits without having to resort to this aid.

A dive from 15,000 feet to a release altitude of 3,000 feet (usual for attacks against defended targets) took about 30 seconds, during which the pilot controlled his aircraft to hold the target in the centre of his reflector sight. Four seconds before the dive bomber passed the pull-out altitude previously set on the contacting altimeter, the latter sounded a horn. When the horn ceased, at release height, the pilot pressed a button on his control column to actuate a powerful spring which returned the elevator trim tab to the neutral position;

* The designation of a German high explosive bomb indicated the type of casing and the weight of the weapon. Thus the SC-250 was a *Spreng Cylindrische* (high explosive, general purpose) bomb weighing 250 kilogrammes; the SD-500 was a *Spreng Dickwand* (high-explosive thick-walled, ie semi-armour piercing) bomb weighing 500 kilogrammes; the PC-1000 was a *Panzerbombe Cylindrische* (armour piercing) bomb weighing 1000 kilogrammes.

Above: During the initial *Blitzkrieg* campaigns the *Luftwaffe* employed all types of fighter and bomber aircraft in the low-level ground attack role. This photograph, taken from a Heinkel 111 over Russia early in 1942, shows men of a Red Army horse-drawn column scurrying for cover before a bombing and strafing attack. The photograph was taken from about twice the height of the telegraph poles, ie about 30 feet./*via Selinger*

Left: The SD-2 fragmentation bomb was unleashed on the first day of the German invasion of Russia. A Ju 88 or a Do 17 could carry up to 360 of these small bombs; a Messerschmitt 109 or a Junkers 87 could carry up to 96. After being released in rapid succession the bombs' casings opened up to form a pair of wings and the individual weapons spun to the ground like sycamore seeds. The bombs could be fused and detonate on impact, after a pre-set delay, or when disturbed. The SD-2 proved extremely effective against troops in the open, aircraft on the ground, or soft-skinned vehicles.

the aircraft, now in a tail-heavy configuration, began automatically to pull itself out of the dive. The pressing of the button had also started the run-down of the bomb-release distributor, and after a set time interval the bombs were released automatically; the special radius arm swung the fuselage bomb down and clear of the propeller disc. After the pull-out the pilot regained control and retracted the dive brakes, opened the throttle, trimmed for level flight and made his getaway.

Ground Attack Tactics

In the context in which it is used in this section, the term 'ground attack' embraces low-level and shallow-dive attacks on tactical ground targets in the battlefield and rear areas, regardless of the type of aircraft making them.

During the campaigns early in the Second World War the *Luftwaffe* possessed only one specialised ground attack aircraft, the Henschel 123 biplane armed with 7.9mm machine guns, 2cm cannon and SC-50 bombs. However, almost all types of aircraft were employed on bombing and strafing work in the battle area, including the Messerschmitt 109 and 110 fighters, the Junkers 87 dive bomber and the Heinkel 111, Junkers 88 and Dornier 17 medium bombers. In each case the aircraft used its gun armament for strafing and carried bombs of up to 250kg in size; large bombs used for low-level attacks were fitted with delayed action fuses, to give the aircraft time to get clear of the lethal fragment zone before the bomb exploded.

During the opening stages of the attack on Russia the *Luftwaffe* unveiled a new type of bomb for ground attack operations, the SD-2 (described above). During attacks with this weapon the aircraft flew at low level singly, in pairs or in threes, releasing their bombs at short intervals to cut swathes of destruction along the ground. A Messerschmitt 109 or a Junkers 87 carried ninety-six of these small bombs, a Junkers 88 or a Dornier 17 could carry up to 360. As well as being very effective against troops in the open, the SD-2 was used against soft-skinned transport and aircraft on the ground. Later these weapons, instead of being released individually from the aircraft, were dropped in containers which opened after release to scatter the bombs over the ground in a pattern; this meant that the bombs could be released in dive or shallow-dive attacks, with less risk to the aircraft from ground fire.

With the increasing ferocity of the battles on the eastern front, and the general ineffectiveness of the horizontal and dive-bombing attacks against Russian tanks, the *Luftwaffe* developed heavy guns for fitting to ground attack aircraft. The Ju 87 was modified to carry two 3.7cm Flak 18 cannon and the Hs 129 to carry a 3cm, 3.7cm or 7.5cm cannon; in each case these weapons fired solid-shot armour-piercing rounds. Used during low level or shallow-dive runs, these heavy cannon proved to be extremely accurate and effective anti-tank weapons; though in the case of the two smaller calibres, attacks had to be made on the more thinly-armoured sides and rear of the tanks. The nature of these strikes, involving a long straight flight path at short range from the enemy positions, meant that losses to anti-aircraft and small arms fire were high; moreover, the performance penalty imposed by the weighty gun installations made the aircraft vulnerable to attack from enemy fighters. As a result

A close-up of a Junkers 87 carrying two 3.7 cm *Flak 18* cannon, for operations in the tank destroyer (*Panzerknacker*) role. Although these aircraft were effective against armoured vehicles, the units operating them suffered heavy losses from ground fire and attacks by enemy fighters./*via Obert*

the gun-armed tank destroyer (*Panzerknacker*) soon fell out of favour and saw little operational use after the spring of 1944.

From the early part of 1944 ground attack versions of the Focke Wulf 190 bore the brunt of the *Luftwaffe* operations in this role, attacking targets with 2cm cannon and 13mm machine guns, 250, 500, 1,000 and 1,800kg bombs, SD-2 and SD-4 cluster weapons (the latter a shaped-charge device for use against tanks) and finally, during the closing months of the war, with *Panzerschreck* and *Panzerblitz* rocket projectiles.

During the last few months of the war there was a resurgence in the use of the Junkers 87, in the night ground attack (*Nachtschlacht*) role. During these operations, usually against targets in the battlefield area, the bombers made a low level approach and climbed to altitudes around 5,000 feet to bomb, then returned to low level for their homebound flight; thus these sorties could be considered more as medium-level horizontal bombing than ground attack.

The final phase of the war also saw the twin-jet Messerschmitt 262 used in small numbers as a ground attack aircraft; in this role it usually carried a bomb load of one SC-500 or two SC-250s. For their initial operations in the Me 262 pilots had strict orders not to fly over enemy territory at altitudes below 4000 metres (about 13,000 feet), to reduce the risk of these new aircraft being shot down and falling into enemy hands; but this limitation made it almost impossible for them to find and hit small targets in the battlefield area. Later the order was rescinded and the Me 262s made shallow (30°) dive attacks from altitudes around 15,000 feet, releasing their bombs at about 3,000 feet. They also carried out low level strafing, though in this case the low velocity of the MK 108 3cm cannon made it necessary to approach to within 400 yards of the target if reasonable accuracy was to be achieved. The high-speed Me 262 was useful in that it alone provided the *Luftwaffe* with a daylight ground attack capability during the closing months of the war, one which was not vulnerable to interception by Allied fighters; but in general the accuracy of the attacks by these aircraft was poor, and they achieved little.

Anti-Shipping Tactics

During anti-shipping operations it was the type of weapon used that dictated the tactics. Early in the war the German dive bombers engaged ships at sea using methods and weapons similar to those employed against targets on land. These tactics were appropriate so long as the strategic situation forced Allied ships to operate in areas close to the German land bases; from the early part of the war, however, the Allied navies learnt from bitter experience that the survival of their vessels depended upon their giving the enemy airfields a wide berth. On the German side the need to attack ships at progressively longer ranges dictated the use of larger aircraft, which in their turn were unable to carry out dive-bombing attacks. In general, horizontal bombing attacks on moving ships from medium or high level using conventional bombs were ineffectual.

At the outbreak of the Second World War, the *Luftwaffe* possessed no bomber able to carry out attacks more than 600 miles from its base. To correct this deficiency the Focke Wulf 200 *Kondor* airliner was modified into a bomber and pressed into service. In its new role the *Kondor* carried five SC-250 bombs

Top: During the latter half of the war the Focke Wulf 190 equipped the majority of the German ground attack units. The aircraft depicted, an F-8 of *Schlachtgeschwader 10*, was operating in Hungary during the winter of 1944–1945; it carries the markings of the Adjutant of the *I. Gruppe.* Under the fuselage may be seen a blunt-nosed bomb container, probably housing SD-2 or SD-4 cluster weapons./*via Obert*

Above: The Messerschmitt 262 was the first turbo-jet powered aircraft in the world to become operational; in July 1944 a small *Kommando* belonging to *Kampfgeschwader 51* began flying these aircraft in the fighter-bomber role against Allied ground forces, from its base at Juvincourt in France. In this photograph a pair of fighter-bombers of *KG 51* are seen taking off; under the nose of each, two SC-250 bombs are just visible./*via Dierich*

and had a radius of action of nearly 1,000 miles. During 1940 and 1941 these aircraft flew singly on armed reconnaissance sorties between Bordeaux/Merignac in France and Stavanger/Sola in Norway, in a wide arc clear of the British Isles, attacking shipping encountered on the way. At that time the Royal Navy was so short of escort vessels that convoys frequently set sail with only one or two small warships to cover them. As a result the marauding *Kondor* aircraft achieved a degree of success far beyond either their limited numbers, or their intrisic qualities as a bomber. These fragile converted airliners were able to make deliberate attacks at mast-level on the almost defenceless merchant ships, with little risk to themselves. The German pilots would release their bombs 'by eye', and at that level they stood a good chance of getting at least one or two hits out of a stick of five bombs. It was all too good to last, and of course it did not. Gradually the provision of short range air defence weapons for merchantmen, and more and more escorts to cover them, made the mast-level attacks increasingly hazardous for the German aircraft and crews. *Kondor* losses began to rise alarmingly, the number of successes slumped, and the aircraft was relegated to the straight maritime reconnaissance role.

A further deficiency in the *Luftwaffe* at the outbreak of the war was the lack of both an effective aerial torpedo and a modern aircraft which could carry it. Not until the early part of 1942 were these shortcomings made good, when the First *Gruppe* of *KG26* became operational with He 111s modified to carry the F5B torpedo; only then did the German torpedo bomber force become a force to be reckoned with in the Allied calculations.

For a typical attack on a convoy, *KG26* would employ between twenty and forty torpedo bombers. They would approach their target in loose Vics of between six and ten aircraft, with two miles between Vics, flying at the He 111's most economical cruising speed of 165mph at an altitude of about 150 feet. In any attack on ships moving in open water an important participant is the shadowing aircraft; without its help the attacking force would at best have to attack without the advantage of surprise, and at worst might fail to find its quarry at all. The Blohm und Voss 138 flying boat was often used as a shadower; it would orbit convoys just out of reach of their defending guns and, when the attacking force was near, radiate signals on which the formation leader could home.

For their run-in the torpedo bombers would usually open out into a line abreast formation with about 300 yards between aircraft, and each crew would select a ship for attack. The Heinkel 111 carried two torpedoes, which were usually aimed at the same target during the same run; the port weapon was released first, followed shortly afterwards by the starboard. Aerial torpedoes were most sensitive to dropping conditions: if they were released at too high a speed or from too low an altitude they were liable to 'belly flop' and bounce off the surface of the sea, often damaging their internal mechanism in the process; released from too high an altitude or at too low an airspeed they were liable to 'nose dive' and go too deep to recover. The optimum launch conditions for the F5B torpedo were from an aircraft flying straight and level at a speed of 170mph and a height of 150 feet; the torpedo then entered the water at an ideal 12 degrees to the horizontal. The best range for the F5B was 1,000 yards from

Top: During 1940 and 1941 the Focke Wulf 200 *Kondor* achieved considerable success during low-level bombing attacks on Allied merchant shipping in the Atlantic. The example depicted belonged to *1./KG 40.*

Above: German armourers moving an SC-250 bomb into position, prior to raising it into the ventral bomb bay of a Focke Wulf 200. On its nose the aircraft carries the 'World-in-a-Ring' badge of *Kampfgeschwader 40.*

Top: The Henschel 293 was the first command guided missile to be used in action. In this photograph two of these weapons are seen fitted under a Focke Wulf 200. The Hs 293 had a wing span of just over 10 feet and carried a 1,100 pound warhead; after launch the rocket motor under the fuselage accelerated the missile to a speed of about 370mph, then it cut and the weapon coasted on to the target.

Above: Not until the beginning of 1942 did the *Luftwaffe* possess an effective torpedo-bomber force, when the Heinkel 111 became operation with the F5B torpedo; both the aircraft and the weapon are depicted in this photograph. The F5B was 16 feet 4 inches long and had a diameter of $17\frac{1}{2}$ inches; with a 440 pound warhead it had a water speed of 33 knots and a maximum effective running distance against a moving ship of about 1,000 yards./*via Schliephake*

the target; the minimum range, allowing the torpedo to settle on its run and arm itself, was about 650 yards. This torpedo had a water speed of 33 knots, and carried a 440 pound warhead.

After releasing the torpedo at the optimum launch range, the aircraft had insufficient time to complete a turn before passing the target ship; so the usual escape tactics were to accelerate straight past the convoy, flying as low as possible, and begin evasive jinking when past the last ship.

Against powerfully defended convoys, German torpedo bombers sometimes attempted dusk or night attacks. In the former case the bombers would plan their run-in from the dark side of the convoy, and aim to catch the ships as they were silhouetted against the light part of the sky. For night attacks, flares had first to be dropped on the opposite side of the convoy to that being attacked; but this required a high degree of co-ordination between the illuminating and the attacking forces and was seldom successful.

When compared with its cost in terms of training and material, the German torpedo bomber force achieved little. Apart from one notable exception, when on September 13th 1942 forty He 111s torpedoed eight ships in convoy PQ 18 during a single sharp attack, successes were few; the tactical constraints on the release of torpedoes were too great, the opportunities to use them were too rare, and from the beginning of 1943 the convoys were usually too well-protected by fighters, for it to be otherwise.

For the *Luftwaffe* to achieve any worthwhile destruction of Allied shipping a weapon altogether more effective than the torpedo was now required; by the middle of 1943 two such were ready for action, the Henschel 293 glider bomb and the Fritz-X guided bomb.

The first of the new weapons to enter service was the Henschel 293 glider bomb, in August 1943. With a wing span of just over 10 feet, it resembled a small aeroplane; its nose carried a warhead weighing 1,100 pounds. After release from the parent aircraft, a liquid fuel rocket motor under the missile's fuselage accelerated it to a speed of approximately 370mph. After twelve seconds running the rocket motor cut, and the missile coasted on in a shallow dive, accelerating slowly towards its target. The range of the weapon depended upon the altitude from which it was released; for example, the effective range was about five miles if the launching aircraft was at 4,500 feet. The tail of the Hs 293 carried a bright flare to enable the observer in the parent aircraft to follow its progress in flight; he operated a small joy-stick controller to transmit the appropriate left-right-up-down signals to the missile. Under this system, known as 'command-to-line-of-sight' in modern terminology, the observer steered the missile until its tracking flare appeared to be superimposed upon the target, and held it there throughout the flight. With an impact speed of only about 450mph the Hs 293 had little penetrative capability, and was intended for use mainly against merchant ships or lightly-armoured warships.

The second of the new weapons was the Fritz-X guided bomb, similarly radio-controlled but otherwise radically different. Intended for use against heavily-armoured warships, it resembled an ordinary free-fall bomb except that it carried four stabilising stub-wings mid-way along its body. Weighing 3,100 pounds, the weapon was released from altitudes between 16,000 and

A typical attack using the Henschel 293 glider bomb. The range of the parent aircraft from the target at the time of missile launch varied between 4,000 and 20,000 yards, giving a missile flight time of between 30 and 110 seconds. During the final part of its flight the missile was radio controlled to stay on the line of sight between the aircraft and the target.

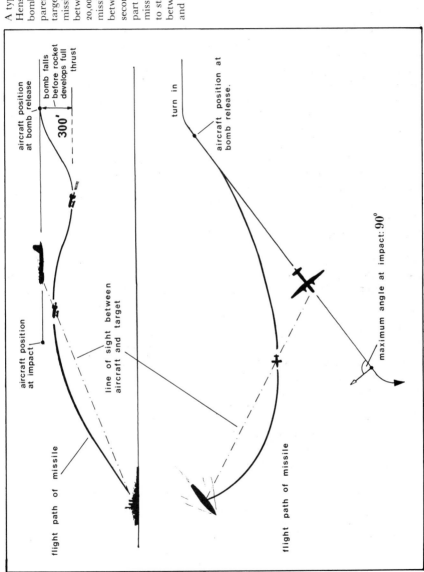

aircraft position at bomb release

bomb falls before rocket develops full thrust

300'

aircraft position at impact

line of sight between aircraft and target

flight path of missile

turn in

aircraft position at bomb release.

maximum angle at impact: 90°

flight path of missile

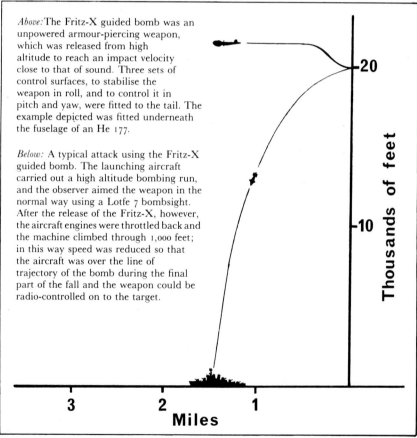

Above: The Fritz-X guided bomb was an unpowered armour-piercing weapon, which was released from high altitude to reach an impact velocity close to that of sound. Three sets of control surfaces, to stabilise the weapon in roll, and to control it in pitch and yaw, were fitted to the tail. The example depicted was fitted underneath the fuselage of an He 177.

Below: A typical attack using the Fritz-X guided bomb. The launching aircraft carried out a high altitude bombing run, and the observer aimed the weapon in the normal way using a Lotfe 7 bombsight. After the release of the Fritz-X, however, the aircraft engines were throttled back and the machine climbed through 1,000 feet; in this way speed was reduced so that the aircraft was over the line of trajectory of the bomb during the final part of the fall and the weapon could be radio-controlled on to the target.

20

10

Thousands of feet

3   **2**   **1**

Miles

21,000 feet; it was unpowered, and simply accelerated under gravity to reach an impact speed close to that of sound. The Fritz-X was aimed using a bomb-sight, like a normal bomb, and the observer transmitted correction signals to bring the tracking flare over the target only during the final part of its trajectory. When attacking with the Fritz-X the launching aircraft, almost invariably Dornier 217s, made individual bombing runs. After the missile was released, the engines were throttled back and the aircraft was climbed through 1,000 feet; in this way speed was reduced from 290mph to 165mph, to ensure that the observer was lined up with the missile and the target and was able to control it during the final 10–15 seconds of flight.

Although their operating requirements were less difficult to meet than were those of the torpedo, the two stand-off missiles did not enable the German bombers to attack Allied shipping with impunity. The need for a medium or high altitude approach, and straight and level flight during the bombing run and subsequent guidance phase of the missile, made the launching aircraft vulnerable to fighter attack; and if the launching aircraft could be forced to evade after the missile had been released but before it had reached its target, the attack almost invariably failed.

Both the Henschel 293 and the Fritz-X achieved spectacular successes during the months immediately following their operational introduction; but within a short time the Allied navies had taken the measure of this new threat and strengthened their fighter defences accordingly. Thereafter the new guided missiles, and for that matter the *Luftwaffe* anti-shipping forces, achieved little.

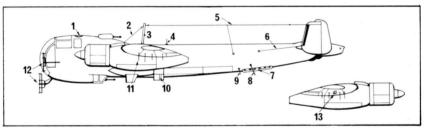

Radio and radar aerials fitted to a Dornier 217. This diagram is intended to enable the reader to identify the various aerials fitted to German bombers, and does not show a typical fit for any particular role. The majority of Do 217s carried Nos 1,2,3,4,5,8 and 9. The key is as follows: (*1*) Suppressed aerial for *Peril Geraet 6*, a navigational direction finder. (*2*) Wire aerial for *FuG 16ZY* VHF R/T and navigational equipment. (*3*) Post used as aerial for the *FuBl 2* blind airfield approach equipment. (*4*) Fixed loop aerial for the FuG 16ZY navigational equipment. (*5*) Wire aerial for *FuG 10* HF radio. (*6*) Wire aerial for the *FuG 203* equipment, which transmitted the radio guidance signals to the Fritz-X guided bomb. (*7*) 'Towel Rail' aerial for the *FuBl 2*. (*8*) Tube through which was lowered the trailing aerial for the FuG 10. (*9*) Whip aerial for the *FuG 25a* Identification Friend or Foe equipment. (*10*) Aerial in the tail of the Fritz-X guided bomb, with which the FuG 230a receiver in the missile picked up the guidance signals from the FuG 203. (*11*) Rod aerials for the *FuG 217R* tail warning radar (four under each wing). (*12*) Transmitter aerial (under nose) and receiver aerials (on each side of nose) for the *FuG 200* ship-search radar. (*13*) Horizontal dipole aerials for the FuG 101a radio altimeter, one for the transmitter and one for the receiver (under starboard wing only).

Top: The Blohm und Voss 138C three-engined flying boat was used for long range oversea reconnaissance missions sometimes lasting over fourteen hours./*Selinger*

Above: BV 138 of *3. Staffel* of *Kuestenfliegergruppe 406* being launched from the catapult ship *Friesenland* moored in Tromso Fjord. Catapult launching enabled the flying boats to get airborne carrying their maximum fuel load./*via Heise*

Top: The Messerschmitt 323 six-engined heavy transport entered service late in 1942 and saw considerable service on the Mediterranean and eastern fronts./*via Schliephake*

Above: A 15cm field artillery piece and half-track towing vehicle, together weighing over ten tons, being loaded into an Me 323. The aircraft could transport such a load a distance of about 300 miles, allowing normal operational fuel reserves./*via Schliephake*

5
Airborne Assault
Operations

Airborne assault is the term used to describe those offensive operations where troops are transported with their equipment by air and are dropped or landed ready for almost immediate action. During the early part of the Second World War the *Luftwaffe* pioneered the operational use of all three techniques by which airborne assault is possible: air landing, parachute dropping, and glider transport. In the German armed services almost all parachute and glider-borne assault troops belonged to the *Luftwaffe*; army units could be used for air landing operations.

Air Landing Operations

During air landing assault operations, the troops were flown directly into action on board aircraft which landed in areas which had yet to be cleared of the enemy. This method had several advantages: no special training was necessary for the troops used; the men were delivered in concentrated groups with their weapons and were ready for almost immediate action on landing; and the transporting aircraft could carry loads much greater than those they could drop by parachute – though rapid unloading was still essential and the need for this reduced the practical payload of the aircraft to below their theoretical maximum. The sole, but often overriding, disadvantage of this form of airborne assault operation was the risk at which it placed the transport aircraft.

The first and only large-scale air landing assault operation mounted by the *Luftwaffe* was during the invasion of Holland in May 1940; on that occasion *Fliegerdivision 7* and the 22nd Infantry Division were put down in the Rotterdam and The Hague areas respectively. Both units succeeded in causing considerable disruption of the defences, but only at a heavy cost in transport aircraft, which had to operate off airstrips under fire from Dutch artillery. It was these air landing operations that claimed the majority of the 170 Junkers 52s destroyed, and the similar number seriously damaged, out of the 430 committed to action during this first week of the campaign in the west.

Parachute Operations

Compared with air-landed troops, parachute troops could be put down with far less risk to the transporting aircraft. On the other hand, the men were not ready to go into action immediately on reaching the ground, there was the risk of troops being scattered over a wide area, and the loads the aircraft were able to drop by parachute were considerably less than the maximum they could carry. On operations the Junkers 52 carried twelve paratroops, which meant that a *Staffel* of twelve aircraft was necessary to lift a *Kompanie* of 144 men.

During paratroop dropping operations the Junkers 52s would make their approach flights in Vics of three aircraft, cruising at 150mph. As they neared the dropping zone the aircraft would close formation until they were 60 yards apart, descend to 400 feet above the ground and reduce speed to 100mph. On the signal to jump the troops went out of the single door on the port side of the aircraft, at approximately one-second intervals. The parachutes were deployed by static lines 20 feet long, and each man fell about 90 feet before the canopy was fully open; thereafter the descent was at 16 feet per second, giving a time in the air of just over twenty seconds for a jump from 400 feet. During the descent each man was about 16 feet below and 150 feet behind his successor. So if a tight formation was held by the transports, the 36 men from the three Junkers 52s arrived spread over an area 120 yards by 500 yards.

Up to and including the invasion of Crete, the only weapons normally carried on the person of the German paratrooper during his jump were a large jack-knife and a 9mm Luger automatic pistol with two extra eight-round magazines. Men in the first waves to land did carry hand grenades, however, and a few dropped with their machine carbines. At the same time as the paratroopers were leaving by the door each Ju 52 released four containers, each weighing about 300 pounds, with the men's personal weapons. Since a great deal might depend upon these weapons being brought into action quickly, the containers were brightly coloured for location and identification and were fitted with quick-release catches for rapid opening. They carried rifles, machine guns, mortars and anti-tank rifles. Heavier weapons were flown in under the fuselages of other Ju 52s, and dropped using clusters of three or four parachutes; those transported in this way included the 2.8cm anti-tank rifle, the 2cm anti-tank/anti-aircraft gun and the 7.5cm light infantry gun.

Glider Operations

Glider-borne troops combined the advantages of air landed and parachute troops, in that the men could be set down in concentrated groups ready for action almost immediately, on terrain on which other aircraft could not land, all without subjecting the towing aircraft to any hazard. If required for tactical reasons, for example to make a silent approach to achieve surprise, gliders could be released at considerable distances from their objective; for example, the DFS 230 could glide 35 miles if released at 10,000 feet in still air, or 50 miles if it had the advantage of a 40mph tail wind. The main disadvantage of this form of assault operation was that the glider itself almost invariably suffered damage which prevented its re-use.

During the large-scale glider assault operations mounted by the *Luftwaffe* the tugs used were Junkers 52s; when employed in this way, the towing aircraft carried no payload. Each Ju 52 towed a single glider, and the tugs usually flew in Vics of three cruising at 110mph. Tow rope lengths varied between 200 and 400 feet, the shorter ropes being used during operations from short airstrips. Once released, the DFS 230 had an optimum gliding speed of about 70mph, depending upon the load carried; its landing speed was about 40mph and its landing run was usually reduced to about 20 yards by an improvised brake consisting of barbed wire wound round the landing skid.

The only type of glider used during assault operations up to and during the invasion of Crete was the DFS 230. The following figures, taken from official *Luftwaffe* schedules, illustrate typical assault loads which could be carried by the DFS 230 in addition to the pilot (who was trained as an infantryman):

4 riflemen
1 machine-gun, with crew of 3 and 2,200 rounds of ammunition
1 handcart
3,000 rounds of rifle ammunition
1 box hollow charge anti-tank grenades
Total 2,350 pounds

9 riflemen
1 field radio
3,000 rounds of rifle ammunition
Total 2,200 pounds

1 mortar with a crew of 5 and ten boxes of mortar bombs
2 riflemen
1 handcart
Total 2,100 pounds

Once the airborne assault troops were on the ground, they operated as light infantry, with all the limitations that went with a lack of heavy supporting weapons. Moreover, although their air transport had conferred upon them great strategic mobility, once they had landed their shortage or lack of vehicles meant that tactically they were almost immobile. For details of German infantry tactics and weapons see *German Army Handbook* by W. J. K. Davies (Ian Allan Ltd).

Above: During the airborne assault operations mounted by the *Luftwaffe*, the Junkers 52 was used almost to the exclusion of all other transport types. In this photograph this aircraft is seen in the paratroop dropping role, in which it carried 12 paratroopers. The man who has just left the door can be seen still connected to the aircraft by the static line which will pull the bag away from his parachute; note the static lines and bags used by previous paratroopers, flapping in the airflow against the rear fuselage./*via Schliephake*

Below: The DFS 230 was the only transport glider used by the *Luftwaffe* during its large-scale airborne assault operations. In addition to the pilot, who was trained as an infantryman, this machine carried a payload of men and weapons of up to 2,400 pounds./*IWM*

6
Pilot Training

'The best form of "welfare" for the troops is a sound training.'

Erwin Rommel

The period of training given to new pilots was steadily shortened during the course of the Second World War; the description below may be considered representative of the situation during the latter half of 1941.

For the prospective pilot joining the *Luftwaffe* from civilian life, the first step was a spell of six months at a *Fliegerersatzabteilung* or recruit training depot; this was the equivalent to the 'square-bashing' or 'boot camps' in other air forces. There the main emphasis was on drill and physical training, and the air aspect was introduced only in elementary lectures on the principles of wireless and map reading.

Having completed this initial training, the student pilot moved to a *Flugan-waerterkompanie*, where he spent up to two months studying general aeronautical subjects. Thus prepared, he moved to an *A/B Schule* (elementary flying school) where he flew light aircraft such as the Klemm 35, the Focke Wulf 44 and the Buecker 131. For his A_2 licence the pupil received instruction in aerodynamics, aeronautical engineering, elementary navigation, meteorology, flying procedures and training in the reception of morse. For his B licence he flew higher-performance aircraft like the Arado 66, the Gotha 145 and the Arado 76, heavier aircraft like the Junkers W 33 and W 44 and the twin-engined Focke Wulf 58, and obsolescent combat types such as the He 51, the Ar 65 and the Hs 123. On successful completion of his B_2 training the candidate had between 100 and 150 hours flying time, and received his *Luftwaffenflugzeugfuehrerschein* (pilot's licence) and his *Flugzeugfuehrerabzeichen* (pilot's wings).

Those pilots selected for single-engined fighters or dive-bombers now went straight to the respective specialist schools for training in these roles.

Prospective twin-engined fighter, bomber and reconnaissance pilots went on to the C Flying Schools, where they received a further 50 to 60 hours flying during a course of some six months' duration. These pilots were given ground training in advanced aeronautical subjects, and flew obsolescent operational types such as (in the case of bomber pilots) early versions of the He111, the Ju52, the Ju86 and the Do17. When he qualified at the C School the pilot received his ELF* or advanced pilot's licence. He was now able to fly his aircraft by day or by night with reasonable proficiency, had limited training in instrument flying, and could perform simple cross-country navigational flights under fair weather conditions.

On leaving the C School, the twin-engined fighter pilots went to their specialist school; the bomber and reconnaissance pilots were sent for 50 to 60 hours extra training in blind-flying, before moving to their specialist schools.

At the various specialist training establishments (Fighter, Bomber, Twin-engined Fighter, Dive-bomber and Reconnaissance) the pilots to fly multi-seat aircraft joined up with their crews. Combined crew training began, flying in operational types of the latest design. In general the exercises engaged in at the specialist schools were similar to those flown by bomber and reconnaissance pilots at the C Schools, but the night and cross-country flights were of longer duration and were undertaken in less favourable weather. On completion of their training at the specialist school, the crew usually remained together and was sent to an operational unit.

An important point to note is that during the initial part of the war the role of the observer (*Beobachter*) in a multi-seat aircraft was not so close to that of navigator as the literal English translation of the term might suggest. In fact the observer was trained as an aircraft captain, having flown as a pilot up to C standard before moving to the observers' school for a nine months' course (where he received further training in blind flying as well as navigation). Soon after the outbreak of the war the rule of the observer being the aircraft captain was gradually relaxed; from the beginning of 1942 observer training steadily deteriorated, until by 1944 it was down to five months, with little pilot training.

Having passed through their respective specialist training schools, the crews were sent to *Ergaenzungs* (operational training) units attached to the various operational *Geschwader* or *Gruppen*. Here the crews learnt the tactical methods peculiar to the operational units they were later to join. As well as providing operational training, the *Ergaenzungs* units served as holding posts for trained crews until they were required by the front-line units.

From the time he joined the *Luftwaffe* until he arrived at his *Ergaenzungs* unit, a fighter or dive-bomber pilot had received about thirteen months training with 150 to 200 flying hours; a bomber or reconnaissance pilot had received respectively twenty months and 220 to 270 hours. It must be stressed, however, that these figures refer only to men who had passed through the system prior to the beginning of 1942. For in that year the *Luftwaffe* training organisation, efficient and smooth-running at the beginning of the war, began to crack under the strain exerted upon it.

The Battle of Britain had been the first major setback for the *Luftwaffe*, but in the main the losses in trained crews were made good by drawing upon the reserves already available within the service. Moreover, the comparatively low casualty rate during the first half of 1941 enabled the remaining gaps in the ranks to be filled without placing undue strain on the training organisation.

* *Erweiterter Luftwaffenflugzeugfuehrerschein.*

The Focke Wulf 44 *Stieglitz*, primary trainer./*via Schliephake*

The relentless rate of losses from the beginning of the Russian campaign, however, made demands which the flying training organisation found almost impossible to meet; during the first six months of the offensive *Luftwaffe* casualties in aircrew, of all categories from all causes in all theatres, amounted to some 2,200 men; during the second six months an almost exactly equal number of men were lost.

The campaign in Russia also brought more direct forms of pressure on the flying training organisation. Early in 1942 many Ju52 aircraft, together with their instructor pilots, were removed from the C, blind-flying and bomber schools and sent to Russia to supplement the fleet of air transports engaged in flying supplies to the German troops cut off at Demjansk and Cholm. Owing to actual losses and shortages at the front line units, many of the instructors and aircraft were never returned to the training organisation. Later in the year the pace of air operations in the east led to a shortage of aviation fuel throughout the *Luftwaffe*; again, it was the flying training schools that suffered.

The shortages of instructors, suitable aircraft and fuel threw out of gear the training programme for bomber and reconnaissance crews; in the short term there was a surplus of partially-trained pilots from the A/B Schools, but at the same time a lack of trained crews available at the *Ergaenzungs* units. In July 1942 General Kuehl, the Director of Training, brought to Goering's notice the fact that the shortages were leading to an impossible situation at the C Schools. As was so often the case, the Reichsmarschall had a glib answer: he ordered that the C Schools should be disbanded, and their functions taken over by the *Ergaenzungs* units. This proved to be beyond the capacity of the latter, however, for they had insufficient aircraft or instructors to cope with this sudden influx of pupils; so, in their turn, the *Ergaenzungs* units farmed out many of them to the operational *Gruppen* for training. The net result of this confused situation was that the general standard of training of new crews for the bomber and long-range reconnaissance units fell so low that operational efficiency began to suffer.

During 1943 the new Director of Training, Generalleutnant Kreipe, was able to slow the rate of deterioration of his organisation. But simple expedients, like the introduction of short glider courses to provide initial flying experience for pilots, could not make up for the perennial shortages of good instructors, modern aircraft and, above all, fuel.

By the beginning of 1944 German fighter pilots were joining their operational units with only about 160 hours flying training; this compared with more than double that figure for their counterparts in the RAF and the USAAF. During the first half of 1944 the *Luftwaffe* day fighter units suffered debilitating losses at the hands of the better-trained American escort fighter pilots, whose P-51B Mustangs could in any case out-perform the best fighters the Germans then had in service; during this period the home-defence units lost some 2,000 pilots killed, missing or wounded. When the *Luftwaffe* training organisation tried to make good these heavy casualties with similar numbers of new pilots, the result was a vicious circle: the ill-trained replacement fighter pilots were no match for their opponents and suffered heavy losses, and their places in the front line were taken by new pilots who had had a more hurried training and were even less of a match for their opponents. During the late spring standards fell yet further, when the B flying schools were disbanded. Fighter pilots were now sent into action with only about 112 hours flying, made up as follows: A School, 2 hours glider flying and 50 hours powered flying on elementary types; Fighter School, 40 hours; *Ergaenzungs* Fighter *Gruppe*, 20 hours. Moreover, the so-called *Windhund* programme, which provided for the hasty conversion of ex-bomber pilots by giving them 20 hours flying in fighters, resulted in a stream of pilots little better able to stand up to the enemy.

In September 1944 the *Luftwaffe* flying training organisation received its death blow. With the systematic wrecking of the German synthetic fuel industry by Allied strategic bombers, aviation fuel production fell so far beneath *Luftwaffe* requirements that operations had to be curtailed. In such a climate the training schools, always the poor relation, could not survive long. First the elementary and many of the specialist schools were closed then, as the last of the trainees passed through, the specialist fighter schools were also disbanded and their instructors sent to the front. By February 1945 the *Luftwaffe* aircrew training organisation had, to all intents and purposes, ceased to exist.

Arado 66, advanced trainer./*via Schliephake*

7
The Flak Arm

Compared with other nations, the Germans were lavish in their deployment of anti-aircraft artillery: at the outbreak of the Second World War the *Luftwaffe* had nearly a million men, or almost two-thirds of its manpower, serving in its *Flak** arm; during the course of the war their numbers gradually increased until at the peak, in the autumn of 1944, about 1,250,000 men and women – about half the *Luftwaffe* personnel – were so employed. For this reason the *Flak* arm merits considerable coverage in any balanced account of the *Luftwaffe*. The German army and navy also possessed their own *Flak* units, though on a considerably smaller scale than the air force; together, the anti-aircraft units of the other two services amounted to no more than a quarter of the strength of those of the *Luftwaffe*.

Organisation

The *Flak* arm of the *Luftwaffe* had a two-fold responsibility: firstly, to protect targets in metropolitan Germany; and secondly, to provide air defence for the field armies and, on occasions, fire support against ground targets. This dual role was reflected in the layout of the staff organisations. The highest head-quarters formation was the *Korps* (Corps), which was fully motorised and oper-ated with the field armies; it controlled between two and four *Divisionen* (Divisions). The staff of a *Flak Division* could be either motorised or static; in the former case it might serve under a *Korps* near the front, or in the latter case (usually for home defence) it came under the control of the local *Luftgau* head-quarters. In static defence a *Division* controlled two or more *Brigaden* (brig-ades), each of between two and four *Regimenter* (regiments). A motorised *Division* controlled between two and four *Regimenter*. A *Regiment* normally con-trolled between four and six *Abteilungen* (battalions) in static defence, or about four *Abteilungen* if it was motorised. By the early part of 1945 the *Luftwaffe* pos-sessed seven *Flak Korps* staffs, 29 *Division* staffs, 13 *Brigade* staffs and 160 *Regiment* staffs with subordinated *Flak Abteilungen*.

The basic *Flak* unit was the *Abteilung*, of which there were four main types:

* *Flak*, short for *Fliegerabwehrkannonen* – anti-aircraft guns.

Schwere (heavy), *Leichte* (light), *Gemischte* (mixed, with both heavy and light guns) and *Scheinwerfer* (searchlight). *Abteilungen* were further sub-divided according to their state of motorisation into fully-motorised (*mot*), semi-motorised (*v*) and static (*o*) units. Typically, a static *Abteilung* comprised the following: if Heavy, four *Batterien* (troops); if Light, three or four *Batterien*; if Mixed, three heavy and two light *Batterien*; and if a Searchlight, three or four *Batterien*. Motorised *Abteilungen* contained fewer and smaller *Batterien* than their static counterparts.

Throughout the war there was a steady drain of able-bodied men away from the static home defence *Flak* units and into the field units. In their places came a hotch-potch collection of men and women: *Flak Wehrmaenner*, workers serving in a 'Home Guard' role with local *Flak* units; *Luftwaffehelfern*, 15 and 16 year old schoolboys who were called away from their lessons, or out of their beds at night, to help man the guns; youths from the *Reichs Arbeit Dienst*, the labour service, into which all young men were recruited after leaving school (unless they went directly into a fighting service); *Flak Kampfhelferinnen*, women auxiliaries employed on non-combattant duties at the gun sites; Italian and Hungarian volunteers; and turncoat Russian prisoners employed for labouring tasks. In October 1944 the *14. Flak Division*, responsible for the defence of the Leuna synthetic oil refinery and other vital installations in southern Germany, comprised the following:

Regular *Luftwaffe* Personnel	28,000
Reichs Arbeit Dienst	18,000
Luftwaffehelfen	6,000
Flak Helferinnen	3,050
Hungarian and Italian volunteers	900
Russian prisonners	3,600
Others	3,000
	62,550

Heavy Flak; Weapons and Ammunition

For the purpose of this section, the term 'heavy *Flak*' includes all weapons of calibre 7.5cm and above. Against aircraft these weapons were aimed using a predictor, rather than sights as in the case of the lighter and faster-firing weapons.

The smallest heavy *Flak* weapon produced in quantity in Germany was the 8.8cm. The first version to go into service was the *8.8cm Flak 18*, which was introduced in 1933 and first saw action during the Spanish civil war. Fitted with a semi-automatic breech mechanism, it had a practical rate of fire of 15 rounds per minute. It fired a shell weighing 19.8 pounds with a muzzle velocity of 2,690 feet per second and had an effective engagement ceiling of 26,250 feet. The firing crew comprised a detachment commander and nine men, reduced later in the war to a commander and six men.

The *8.8cm Flak 36* was similar to the *-18* but was fitted on an improved mounting; the *8.8cm Flak 37* resembled the *-36* but carried the dials and fittings for the *Uebertragungsgeraet 37*, a data transmission system which brought fire

The heaviest calibre gun operated by the *Luftwaffe* was the *12.8cm Flak 40*. This photograph shows the *12.8cm Flakzwilling 40* which comprised two such weapons on a common traversing and elevating mounting; the use of these paired guns was confined to the giant *Flak* towers situated in the principal German cities./*Bundesarchiv*

control information directly from the predictor.

The *8.8cm Flak 41* was the first major redesign of this weapon, with a longer and stronger barrel; as a result the muzzle velocity was increased to 3,110 feet per second, which gave an effective engagement ceiling of approximately 35,000 feet. This version incorporated a power rammer and had a practical rate of fire of 20 rounds per minute; the increase in muzzle velocity led to higher barrel temperatures, however, and after every 25 rounds fired the barrel required five minutes to cool. The *8.8cm Flak 41* entered service in 1943.

The *10.5cm Flak 38* was introduced just before the beginning of the Second World War, to provide greater hitting power and a higher engagement ceiling than was possible with the early 8.8cm weapons. It fired a 32.2 pound shell at a muzzle velocity of 2,890 feet per second, to an effective engagement ceiling of 31,000 feet. This weapon incorporated electrical ramming and power-assisted laying, and had a practical rate of fire of 10–15 rounds per minute; it required a crew of nine for normal operation, or eleven if the power rammer could not be used. The *10.5cm Flak 38* was essentially the same as the -*37*, but incorporated a more efficient data transmission system and other minor improvements.

The *12.8cm Flak 40* was produced in response to a requirement for a weapon with even greater hitting power than the 10.5cm pieces; it was the heaviest gun operated by the *Luftwaffe*. It fired a 57 pound shell at a muzzle velocity of 2,890 feet per second and had an effective engagement ceiling of about 35,000 feet. Fitted with powered ramming, elevation and traverse, this weapon had a practical rate of fire of 8–10 rounds per minute. The *12.8cm Flakzwilling 40* comprised two barrels about three feet apart, on a common traversing and elevating mounting; the use of these paired guns was confined to the giant *Flak* towers situated in the principal German cities.

In addition to the above-mentioned heavy *Flak* weapons, the *Luftwaffe* made considerable use of captured anti-aircraft guns. These were issued to many of the auxiliary *Flak* units defending targets in Germany; in addition, the anti-aircraft gun defences in the occupied territories were often left in position after their capture, and manned by German personnel. Normally the captured guns fired their own ammunition, but in some cases they were modified to fire German rounds; examples of this were the Russian 7.62cm and 8.5cm weapons, which were bored out to fire the standard German 8.8cm shell. Captured guns received a German designation, followed by the initial letter of the country of origin; the list opposite contains the more important of the captured heavy anti-aircraft weapons which were impressed into service.

When used against aircraft, heavy *Flak* weapons almost invariably fired time-fused high explosive ammunition. During 1943, in an attempt to produce larger fragments when the shell exploded and thus give a more lethal effect against the tough Allied heavy bombers, the Luftwaffe introduced *gerillt* (grooved) controlled-fragmentation ammunition in 8.8cm and 10.5cm cizes. These shells were grooved on the inside of their casings, so that when the charge exploded the case split into large fragments of a pre-determined size; from a *gerillt* shell these measured about $3\frac{1}{2}$ inches long, $\frac{3}{4}$ inch wide and $\frac{1}{2}$ inch thick, and were far more dangerous to aircraft than the smaller fragments had been. Towards the end of the war increasing numbers of *Brandschrapnel* (incendiary shrapnel)

Equipment	Country of Origin	German Designation
7.5cm AA gun	France	*7.5cm Flak (f)*
3in Vickers AA gun	Britain	*7.5cm Flak Vickers (e)*
7·62cm AA gun	Russia	*7.62cm Flak (r)*
		or *7.62/8.8cm Flak (r)*
7.65cm AA gun	Czechoslovakia	*7.65cm Flak (t)*
8.5cm AA gun	Russia	*8.5cm Flak (r)*
		or *8.5/8.8cm Flak (r)*
9cm AA gun Ansaldo	Italy	*9cm Flak (i)*
3.7in Vickers AA gun	Britain	*9.4cm Flak Vickers (e)*
10.2cm AA gun	Italy	*10.2cm Flak (i)*

shells were fired during engagements; these were thin-walled projectiles, housing 51 small incendiary pellets in the case of the 8.8cm round, and 99 in the 12.8cm round. When the shell reached the altitude at which the time fuse had been set to function, a bursting charge ejected the pellets, which then continued forwards and outwards; these pellets ignited either on leaving the shell or on striking the target, and were intended to pierce the aircraft's fuel tanks and cause fires. Following trials, the Germans considered that against the heavy bomber incendiary shrapnel was considerably more effective than the controlled-fragmentation type of shell, which in its turn had been a major improvement over the earlier non-grooved projectile.

In addition to their normal forms of aircraft-destroying ammunition, the heavy *Flak* units also fired star shells to provide navigational assistance for German fighters or to confuse enemy flare illumination of the target. Typical of these rounds was the *8.8cm Leuchgeschoss* which, on detonation by a simple time fuse, ejected a parachute carrying a white or coloured flare which burnt for about fifteen seconds.

'Scarecrows'

During the course of the war there were frequent reports from Allied bomber crews concerning the German use of the so-called 'Scarecrow' shells. According to one document these took the form of 'an explosion releasing a quantity of smoke, coloured stars and flaming debris, resembling an aircraft which had been destroyed. Distinguishable from the real thing, and apparently not lethal at close range.' The purpose of these explosions was, apparently, to sap the morale of the bomber crews rather than to damage them or their aircraft.

During 1940 the *Luftwaffe* experimented with a type of 8.8cm shell which exploded with an especially bright flash; the intention was that, in addition to the destructive effect of the burst, the flash would prove disconcerting for bomber crews engaged in night attacks. It was soon found, however, that the brighter flash had a negligible effect on either the accuracy of the bombing or the extent of evasive action taken by the bombers; it merely made it more difficult for the German optical range-finder crews to follow their target. As a result this type of ammunition was withdrawn from service after a short time.

69

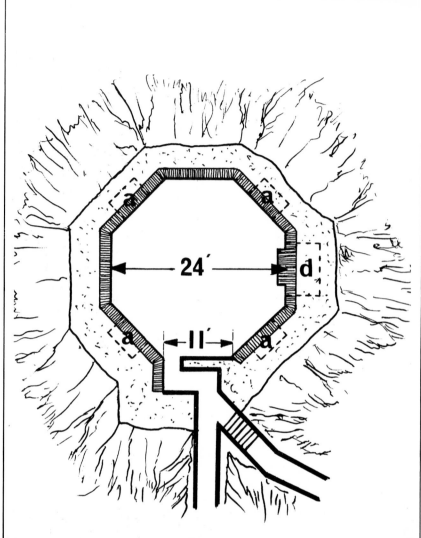

a: Ammunition Stores
d: Dugout

Left: Diagram showing the size and shape of a typical emplacement to take heavy *Flak* weapons of up to and including 10.5cm calibre.

Right: A gunner, wearing one of the perennially scruffy off-white *Drillichzeug* suits worn by *Flak* crews, seen cleaning a 10.5cm shell. Behind him are the racks for the ready-use ammunition./*Wingender via Krueger*

Below: The *Kommandogeraet 40* was the standard German *Flak* predictor during the latter half of the war. The five rings round the range finder give the victory tally claimed by the *Batterie.*/*Wingender via Krueger*

Above: A close-up of the receiver dials of the *Uebertragungsgeraet 37* data-transmission system, mounted on an *8.8cm Flak 37* gun; by keeping the gun position pointers aligned with the pointers carrying the fire-control information from the predictor, the azimuth and elevation layers were able to keep the gun aimed at the calculated future position of the target aircraft./*via Bergander*

Above right: Captured Russian 8.5cm guns, like the one depicted here operating near Dresden, had their barrels bored out and re-lined to enable them to fire the standard German 8.8cm shell, and received the German designation *8.5/8.8cm Flak (r)*. The object on the end of the barrel is a simple cover. This photograph shows clearly the inside of an earth-walled emplacement used for German heavy *Flak*; the numbers round the wall were part of a clock-code for rough alignment of the weapon (12 o'clock equalled north)./*via Bergander*

Above: The standard German radar for use with *Flak* was the *Wuerzburg D*, seen here in a typical shallow emplacement; by means of electrical data transmission equipment, information on the position of the target aircraft could be passed to the predictor. The Wuerzburg had a maximum tracking range of about 15 miles. During its career its spread of operating frequencies expanded from 560–570 megacycles initially to 450–600 megacycles, in a race to circumvent the growing barrage of Allied jamming./*via Heise*

Below: Inside the command post of a *Flak Batterie*, showing the *Malsi* converter which enabled a site without a radar to make use of information from the set of a nearby *Batterie*. The two crew members standing and facing left can be seen wearing the strap-on earphones and throat microphones used to pass and receive information on the target./*via Schliephake*

The author has conducted a lengthy investigation into the phenomenon of the 'Scarecrow' shell, and is convinced that apart from the case mentioned above the *Luftwaffe* made no attempt to use ammunition designed *solely* to affect the morale of enemy aircrew. Nevertheless there is powerful if one-sided evidence that odd effects were seen in the skies over Germany; if these were not produced deliberately, it is of interest to speculate on how they may have occurred accidentally. There are several possibilities. The bursting flash of the largest German *Flak* shell, the 12.8cm, was always very bright and sometimes had a 'catherine wheel' appearance; this effect was, however, a natural result of the large charge and was not deliberate. Furthermore, the pellets from incendiary shrapnel shells could have produced the 'swarm of bees' effect sometimes described. Other unusual phenomena could have been caused by faulty ammunition, possibly the result of sabotage by foreign workers. Star shells, fired either to assist German night fighters or to immitate the British pathfinder markers, could also fail to detonate properly and thus produce peculiar effects. And there can be little doubt that many of the explosions later confidently described as 'Scarecrows' were, in fact, caused by real aircraft blowing up.

Fire Control Equipment for Heavy Flak

The standard German predictor for heavy *Flak* at the beginning of the war was the *Kommandogeraet 36*, and many were still in use when hostilities ceased. This instrument incorporated a rangefinder with a 4 metre baseline; so long as the rangefinder's telescopes were on the target, the predictor produced a continuous flow of information on the future position of the aircraft, in terms of gun bearing, elevation and time-fuse setting for the shells. This instrument could not cope with a turning target, however, and the maximum aircraft ground speed it could accept was about 400mph (easily exceeded by much slower aircraft with a tail wind). Initially the *Kommandogeraet 36* was unable to receive electrical data from radar sets nearby, though later it was modified to do so.

The *Kommandogeraet 40*, which superseded the -*36* in production, was a more compact instrument, able to cope with targets in a steady turn as well as those flying at speeds of up to 670mph; it could receive data transmitted from a radar positioned nearby. The -*40* required an operating crew of only five, compared with the thirteen needed by the earlier model.

In addition to the *Kommandogeraet 36* or -*40* many *Batterien* used the *Kommandohilfsgeraet 35* as a reserve predictor in case the main instrument went out of action. Unlike the main predictors, this auxiliary one could not be corrected for the difference between its position and that of the guns, so it had always to be positioned in the centre of the *Batterie* whose fire it was to control.

During the greater part of the Second World War there were insufficient radar sets for every heavy *Flak Batterie* to have one. To enable *Batterien* without radar to engage targets at night or above cloud, using data from a radar-equipped *Batterie* nearby, the *Malsi* converter was introduced. This device comprised a circular table marked with the *Flak* grid, on which the target information telephoned from the radar was plotted; members of the operating team were then able to convert these plots into fire-control data for the guns of their own *Batterie*. Although *Malsi* converted radar information was better than none at all, the inaccuracies of the system meant that fire laid by this means was considerably less accurate than normal radar-laid fire.

Layout of a Heavy Flakbatterie

During the course of the war many different layouts were used, and the description below must be regarded only as representative. Prior to the outbreak of the Second World War the standard arrangement for a four-gun heavy *Flakbatterie* comprised four guns positioned at the corners of a square with sides of approximately 35 yards, with the command post in the centre. Early in the conflict the command post with the predictors was moved out of the square to a position about 100 yards away from the guns; there the instruments and their operators were outside the area affected by the blast and muzzle flash from the guns. Those *Batterien* covering important targets often had an auxiliary command post, sometimes employing the *Kommandohilfsgeraet 35*; if this was the case the auxiliary command post was situated in the centre of the guns. In addition to its heavy weapons, each *Batterie* had two 2cm guns for self-protection.

At the end of 1941 a policy change resulted in the deployment of six-gun heavy *Batterien*. At existing sites this was effected by placing one of the extra guns at each end of the square; at new sites the six guns were laid out either in a circle, or in a circle of five with a sixth in the centre. Later still eight-gun *Batterien* became common, typically in a circle of seven with the eighth in the centre. When a site had a radar, it was usually located close to the main fire control instruments at the command post.

During 1942 the necessity to concentrate fire against bombers attacking in formation by day, or in compact streams by night, led to the assembly of the so-called *Grossbatterien* – two or even three normal *Batterien* with the same type of weapon, sited close together and firing on data from a common command post. The proportion of heavy *Flak* units grouped into *Grossbatterien* rose steadily during the final three years of the war.

In a few of the very large cities, for example Berlin, Hamburg and Vienna, massive concrete *Flak* towers were constructed. These towers were erected in pairs, the larger one carrying four heavy guns – 10.5cm, 12.8cm or double 12.8cm – and the smaller one containing the associated radar and fire-control equipment; in addition, both types of tower usually mounted 2cm light *Flak* weapons. Apart from providing space for the storage of ammunition, the lower stories of the towers served as air raid shelters and civil defence headquarters.

Within the general scheme of air defence, the Germans attached great importance to the so-called *Eisenbahnflak* (railway *Flak*) units. These comprised both light and heavy *Batterien* with guns and fire-control instruments mounted on railway flats, and were used as a mobile reserve to provide rapid reinforcement for districts where heavy air attacks were anticipated; when deployed, these guns were fired from their flats, which were drawn up in sidings or marshalling yards close to the vulnerable point.

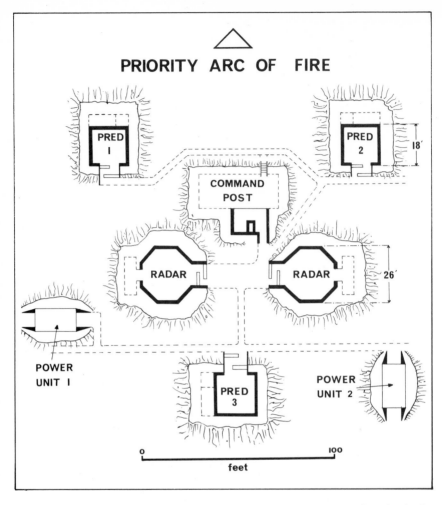

PRIORITY ARC OF FIRE

PRED
1

PRED
2

18′

COMMAND
POST

RADAR

RADAR

26′

POWER
UNIT 1

PRED
3

POWER
UNIT 2

0   100

feet

Above: A close-up of the layout of the fire control instruments for a typical *Grossbatterie*. The third predictor and the second power unit were reserves, in case of failure of the main units.

Above right: A typical command post bunker for a heavy *Flak Batterie*.

Right: Layout of a typical *Flak* tower; the men in front of the entrance door give scale to the massive structure.

76

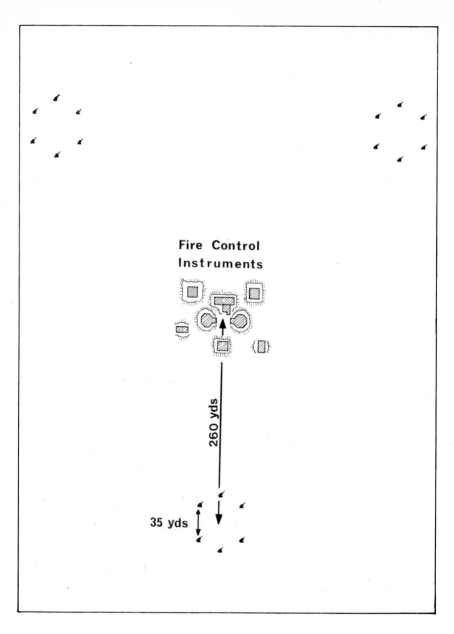

Fire Control Instruments

260 yds

35 yds

The layout of a typical *Grossbatterie*, showing the positioning of the three constituent six-gun *Batterien* in a triangle round their fire control instruments. The centre of each *Batterie* was about 260 yards from the centre of the fire control instruments; the centre of each gun emplacement was about 35 yards from that of its neighbour. When in action, all eighteen guns fired simultaneous salvoes at the single target tracked by the controlling predictor.

Searchlights Operating with Heavy Flak

The most-used searchlight in the *Luftwaffe* at the beginning of the Second World War was the *150cm Flakscheinwerfer 37*. The unit for the deployment of searchlights was the *Abteilung* with three (later four) *Batterien* each with nine (later between twelve and sixteen) lights. During the early war period the searchlights were laid out in a chessboard pattern, with intervals of about three miles between individual lights; this searchlight zone was positioned outside the *Flak* engagement area, in the 'zone of preparation' (see page 80). The lights were assisted in finding their targets by sound locators or, later, by radar.

During 1942 the more powerful *200cm Flakscheinwerfer 40* entered service; usually these were positioned close to the radar of a heavy *Flakbatterie*, so that they could use its information to assist in locating the target. When employed in this way the 200cm searchlight served as the Master Light (*Leitgruppe*), and once it was on the target the three 150cm satellite lights working with it were switched on to 'cone' the aircraft. A typical layout for such a group of four lights comprised the Master Light in the centre, and the three satellite lights at the corners of a triangle each about one-and-a-half miles from the Master. The interval between one Master Light and the next was about 3 miles.

It should be noted that the searchlights constituted an effective method of target defence in their own right: once enveloped in their blinding glare, no bomber crew at medium or high level could possibly carry out an accurate bombing run by night.

Principles of Siting Heavy Flak

So far as the gunners were concerned, enemy bombers could be expected to approach a vulnerable point from any direction; so the gun defences had to be positioned in a circle round the target to be protected. During the early war period the defences were laid out on the assumption that the maximum speed and height of attacking bombers would be 265mph and 20,000 feet; the bombs from such aircraft would carry forward about 4,400 yards after release. A circle or near circle 4,400 yards from the outer edge of the vulnerable point, joining the points of bomb release, was known as the Line of Bomb Release (LBR). *Flak* sites were laid out so that the bombers could be engaged during most or all of their run up to the bomb release point, a period of about 50 seconds. In 50 seconds a bomber flying at a ground speed of 265mph covered about 6,600 yards; so the *Flak* engagement zone ran from 6,600 yards outside the LBR, to the LBR itself. Beyond the *Flak* engagement zone lay the so-called 'zone of preparation', in which the predictors tracked targets and computed the necessary fire-control data for the guns to open fire as soon as aircraft came within range.

Aircraft with a performance lower than the assumed maximum had to cross the calculated LBR to release their bombs, so their engagement presented no problems. Later in the war, when the newer Allied bombers attacked faster and higher than had been allowed for at the time of the establishment of the LBR, the latter was re-calculated to take this into account.

The siting of individual *Batterien* depended on the number available to defend a target. If there were three *Batterien*, they would be laid out in an ap-

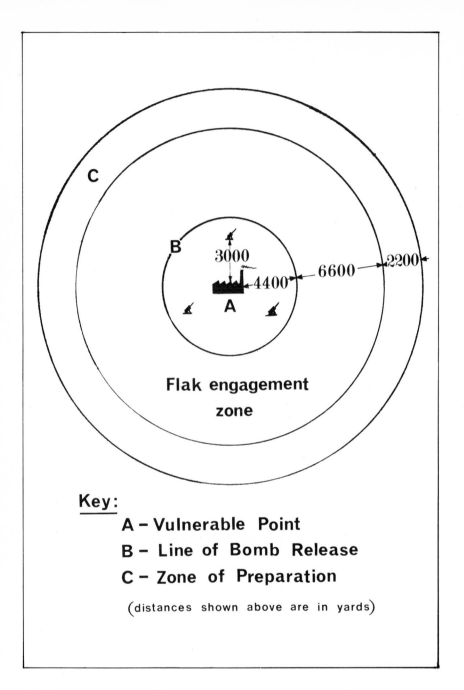

C

B

3000

4400

6600

2200

A

Flak engagement
zone

Key:

A – Vulnerable Point

B – Line of Bomb Release

C – Zone of Preparation

(distances shown above are in yards)

Ideal siting scheme for three *Flak Batterien* to cover a vulnerable point; each *Batterie* is indicated by a single gun symbol.

proximately equilateral triangle, each being about 3,000 yards from the point to be defended; if there were five *Batterien*, four would be sited at the corners of a square about 4,400 yards from the vulnerable point, with the fifth close to the point. Where guns were deployed to cover a large target, such as a city, it was usual to split the latter into several smaller vulnerable areas round which the guns were positioned in the normal way.

Principles for the Engagement of High-flying Aircraft by Heavy Flak

Guns opened fire at their maximum effective range (about 10,000 yards in the case of the *8.8cm Flak 18/36/37*), provided that they had accurate fire-control data from their predictors. Bombers flying singly were engaged as they came within range. If a formation of bombers was to be engaged, the priority target was the aircraft at the head of the formation (unless this had already been allocated to a *Batterie* nearby, in which case a second aircraft in the formation was engaged as well). If a formation was to be engaged with radar-laid fire, there were likely to be several aircraft within the limits of discrimination of the radar; in this case the fire was directed at the centre of the leading formation. All the guns of the *Batterie* engaged the same target aircraft, firing by salvoes as fast as was possible unless a shortage of ammunition decreed otherwise.

It was the responsibility of the Tactical Control Officer (who was usually, though not invariably, the *Batterie* commander) to decide when fire should be shifted to the next target; this was usually when the aircraft being engaged had crossed the Line of Bomb Release.

To ensure smooth engagement of a succession of targets, *Grossbatterien* were equipped with at least two radars and two predictors. The first radar/predictor combination to produce fire-control data on the designated target aircraft controlled the fire of the guns during the initial engagement. While that target was being engaged by the guns, the other radar/predictor combination, and engaged with a minimum of delay. As soon as it had relinquished When the Tactical Control Officer decided to shift fire to the second target he simply switched the guns to the data from the second radar/predictor combination, and engaged with a minimum of delay. As soon as they had relinquished control of the guns, the first radar/predictor combination reverted to the search role and sought out a third target.

Light and Medium Flak: Weapons and Ammunition

The principal automatic weapon used by the German light *Flak* units was the 2cm gun. There were two models, the *2cm Flak 30* and the *-38*, the latter being introduced shortly after the beginning of the war. The *-30* had a practical rate of fire of 120 rounds per minute, while the *-38* could fire 180 rounds per minute. Ballistically the two weapons were identical, each firing a 4-ounce shell at a muzzle velocity of 2,950 feet per second. Ammunition was fed in by means of 20-round magazines. The 2cm gun could be mounted on railway wagons, lorries or tracked vehicles, or on a specially-designed two-wheeled trailer. There was also a special lightweight trailer for use in mountainous country, and when thus fitted the weapon was known as the *2cm Gebirgs Flak 38*.

The *2cm Flakvierling 38* comprised four *2cm Flak 38* on a quadruple mounting,

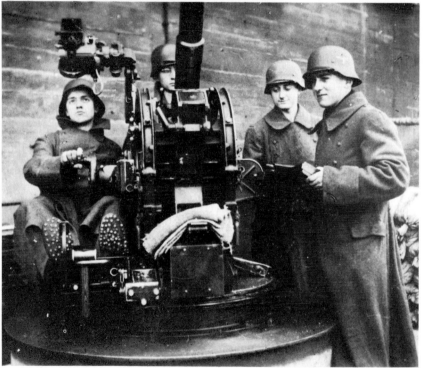

Top: The most-used type of searchlight in the *Luftwaffe* was the *150cm Flakscheinwerfer 37*, seen here in a typical shallow emplacement./*via Schliephake*

Above: The crew pictured with their 2cm gun, static-mounted on a *Flak* tower in Berlin.

The man seated on the left was the azimuth and elevation layer, the two on the right were loaders and the man at the rear was the gun commander. The layer has his foot against the gun-firing pedal./*via Bergander*

which could be either mobile or static. The trigger mechanism was operated by two foot pedals, each of which actuated the triggers of the two diametrically-opposite guns.

The standard medium *Flak* gun used by the Germans was the 3.7cm, designed to provide greater range and hitting power than was possible with the 2cm weapons. The main models produced were the *3.7cm Flak 18,-36 and -43*, and the twin-barrelled *3.7cm Flakzwilling 43*. Ballistically these weapons were identical, each with a practical rate of fire of 80 rounds per minute per barrel, firing 1 pound 5 ounce shells with a muzzle velocity of 2,690 feet per second; the newer models featured improvements to increase mobility. Ammunition was fed in by means of 6-round magazines, clipped into place.

Against aircraft, light and medium *Flak* weapons fired high explosive rounds with percussion fuses; a self-destruction mechanism exploded the shells when they reached their maximum effective range, to prevent their causing damage when they fell to the ground. Both tracer and non-tracer rounds were used.

Fire-control of Light and Medium Flak

The visual sights used for light and medium *Flak* weapons were designed to bring the initial bursts as close to the target as possible, subsequent adjustments being made by the observation of tracer. Up to the end of 1944 one member of the gun crew operated a 1 metre rangefinder and called out the range of the target for setting on the sight; after the end of 1944 the rangefinding crewman was disestablished, and fire was opened on estimated range values and corrected on tracer.

Layout of a Light or Medium Flak Zug

The standard fire unit for light and medium *Flak* weapons was the *Zug* (section) with three guns. A *Batterie* comprised four or five such *Zuege* if equipped with 2cm guns, or three or four *Zuege* if equipped with 3.7cm guns. Early in the war the three guns of a *Zug* were laid out in a triangle having sides of about 250 yards, with the apex toward the vulnerable point; from 1944 the policy was to concentrate weapons, and the spacing was reduced to about 60 yards between guns. A small circular emplacement was often positioned in the centre of the guns, for use by the *Zug* commander.

Principles of Siting Light and Medium Flak

Light and medium *Flak Zuege* were normally sited in the same way as heavy guns, to cover a zone of engagement in front of the Line of Bomb Release. In the case of the lighter weapons, however, the LBR was calculated for aircraft flying at 500 feet at 330mph, which meant that it was about 1,000 yards from the vulnerable point. Thus when both heavy and light weapons were employed in the protection of the same vulnerable point, the heavy weapons were positioned well outside the light *Flak* weapons.

Principles for the Engagement of Low-flying Aircraft by Light or Medium Flak

Against closing targets the effective range of the 2cm gun was about 1,100 yards and that of the 3.7cm gun about 1,600 yards. Since an aircraft flying at 330mph covered 150 yards per second, it can be seen that targets were within range for only a short time. Thus it was important that the guns opened fire against low-flying aircraft as soon as they came within effective range; all the guns of the *Zug* engaged the aircraft that was under fire from the command gun. Because of the lack of proper prediction equipment, only aircraft flying almost directly towards or away from the site could be engaged effectively by light or medium *Flak*.

Light or medium *Flak Zuege* operating from lorries or half-track vehicles were frequently used during the latter stages of the war to protect road convoys from fighter-bomber attack. For a convoy 1,000 yards long three such *Zuege* would usually be provided; one travelled at the front, one in the middle and one at the rear. When engaged in convoy protection the guns had to be ready to fire whilst the vehicles were under way; on each weapon the layer remained in his seat, the guns' magazines were fitted and air sentries were posted. When enemy fighter-bombers were sighted in a threatening position the gun crew making the sighting gave the alarm by opening fire in the direction of the threat. The entire convoy then halted and all personnel except the *Flak* gunners took cover. The individual *Flak Zuege* pulled off the road to the right or the left (if there was room) and the three vehicles of each took up a triangular position in order to avoid firing over one another (and thus interfering with the spotting of tracer). The attackers were then engaged in the normal way.

A *3.7cm Flak* in a simple dug-out emplacement. The gun crew of eight comprised a commander, an azimuth and elevation layer (nearest camera, holding wheel), a range setter, two loaders, two men to pass ammunition clips and a range taker (standing behind gun, supporting his 1 metre rangefinder on his shoulders)./ *IWM*

8
The Fieseler 103
Flying Bomb

The Weapon

The Fieseler 103 flying bomb was known to the Germans as the *Kirschkern* (Cherry Stone), the *Flakzielgeraet* (*Flak* target device) or *Vergeltungswaffe 1* (Revenge Weapon No 1) and to the Allies as the V 1 or 'Doodle-bug'. Its importance in any book on the *Luftwaffe* derives from the fact that following the virtual demise of the German conventional bomber force in mid-1944, owing to the fuel shortage, it was the only strategic bombardment weapon in large-scale operation by that service during the final year of the war. The rival A-4 (V 2) rocket was operated by the German army and is therefore outside the compass of this volume.

The Fi 103 was a small pilotless aircraft with a wing span of 17 feet 6 inches and an overall length of 25 feet 4 inches. With an all-up weight at launch of 4,858 pounds and a wing area of 55 square feet, it had a wing loading of 88 pounds per square foot. The warhead, mounted in the forward end of the fuselage, contained 1,870 pounds of high explosive. The airframe was designed for a single flight lasting a maximum of forty minutes, so its construction was as simple and as cheap as possible. For the most part the structure was built out of thin sheet steel and there was a minimum of sophistication. For example, the main part of the tailplane was formed out of a single piece of .034 inch thick sheet steel, with stiffening strips, which was simply bent over a former and spot-welded along the trailing edge; there were no ribs. The tips of the tailplane were unfinished steel pressings inserted into the ends and spot-welded. There were no fuel pumps; the fuel was forced up to the motor by the simple expedient of pressurising the tank by means of compressed air from spherical containers mounted in the rear fuselage of the missile; the tank itself held 150 gallons of low grade (75 octane) petrol. Similarly, compressed air was used to drive the gyros in the autopilot and also the rudder and elevator control servos (the missile did not have ailerons). The compressed air containers were charged up prior to launch and contained sufficient air for a flight of about 40 minutes. During flight the flying bomb was maintained on its pre-set heading by a magnetic compass, and at its pre-set altitude by a barometric capsule.

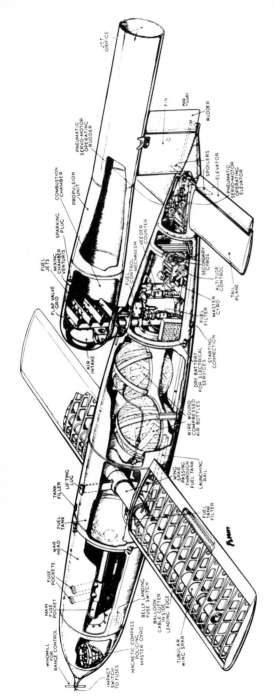

JET ORIFICE

PNEUMATIC SERVO-MOTOR OPERATING RUDDER

FIN

MOD COLLAR

RUDDER

SPOILERS

ELEVATOR

PNEUMATIC SERVO-MOTOR OPERATING ELEVATOR

COMBUSTION CHAMBER

PROPULSION UNIT

SPARKING PLUG

MIXING CHAMBER VENTURIS

FUEL JETS

FUEL CONTROL MECHANISM

VEEDER COUNTER

SECONDARY GYROS

ALTITUDE CONTROL

MASTER GYRO

TAIL PLANE

FLAP VALVE GRID

FUEL FILTER

AIR INTAKE

STARTING CONNECTION

DRY BATTERY FOR ELECTRICAL SERVICES

WIRE WOUND COMPRESSED AIR BOTTLES

WING SPAR PASSING THROUGH FUEL TANK

LAUNCHING RAIL

FUEL TANK FILTER

TANK FILLER

LIFTING LUG

FUEL TANK

WAR HEAD

FUSE POCKETS

MAIN FUSE POCKET

BELLY LANDING FUSE SWITCH

BALLOON CABLE CUTTER INSIDE LEADING EDGE

TUBULAR WING SPAR

WINDMILL FOR RANGE CONTROL

MAGNETIC COMPASS POLICING MASTER GYRO

IMPACT SWITCH TO FUSES

PLANT

Above: Cut-away drawing of the Fieseler 103./*Flight*

Left: Flying bomb in flight.

86

After launch a small windmill vane on the nose of the missile spun in the air-flow, driving a mechanical counter which served as a crude form of milometer; at previously-arranged distances after launch this air log mechanism armed the warhead, switched on the radio transmitter (if one was fitted) and initiated the final dive. The thrust developed by the pulse-jet increased with speed and varied from missile to missile, but was approximately 560 pounds at 400mph.

The Ground Launching Organisation

The unit responsible for the ground launching of the Fi 103 was code-named *Flak Regiment 155 (W)*, later *Flak Gruppe Creil*, during the operations against Britain up to the late summer of 1944*. The *Regiment* was organised along the same general lines as a *Flak* unit, being sub-divided into *Abteilungen, Batterien* and *Zuege*. *Abteilungen I, II, III* and *IV* controlled the firing units, *Abteilung V* the signals personnel. Each of the firing *Abteilungen* comprised four firing and two supply *Batterien*; each firing *Batterie* controlled two *Zuege*, which in turn each controlled two launching sites and their crews. Thus a *Zug* controlled two launchers, a *Batterie* four, a firing *Abteilung* sixteen and the *Regiment* sixty-four launchers.

The crew of a launching site comprised some fifty NCOs and men, divided into seven squads: the assembly squad (*Montagetrupp*), with one NCO and four men; the steering unit assembly squad (*Steuerungstrupp*), with one NCO and two men; the course setting squad (*Einstelltrupp*), one NCO and six men; the ramp squad (*Geschuetztrupp*), one NCO and five men; the fuelling squad (*Lade-trupp*), one NCO and two men; the transport squad (*Transporttrupp*), two NCOs and twenty men; and the NCO site commander and two wireless oper-ators.

The Firing Sequence

The flying bombs arrived at the firing site dismantled, by lorry; the warheads were already in place, however, and the fuel tanks were full. The missiles were unloaded by men of the transport squad, and when they were required for firing they were moved into the assembly room at the site. Initially the flying bomb was assembled, except for its wings, by the assembly squad; then it was passed to the steering unit assembly squad, who charged the compressed air containers and checked the operation of the autopilot and the servos to the con-trol surfaces. The missile was then wheeled into a special non-magnetic build-ing (the *Einstellhaus*), where its assembly was completed and the course setting squad aligned the gyro-compass system.

While the Fi 103 was thus being readied for its first (and last) flight, the ramp squad was preparing the launcher. Immediately after the discharge of the pre-vious bomb the ramp was hosed down, to remove all traces of the potentially dangerous chemicals used during the launch; for this work the men of the ramp squad wore rubber boots and protective clothing. When the hosing was complete, the slideway running up the ramp was greased. The launching ramp itself was 48 metres (about 156 feet) long and elevated to a height of five metres (about 16 feet) at one end; it was constructed from eight 6-metre sections, each

* Air-launched Fi 103 operational methods are described on page 36.

of which was supported at its higher end by an A-frame resting on a concrete base. Running up the length of the ramp was the firing tube 30cm (11½ inches) in diameter, along the top of which was a slot 15mm (just over ½ inch). wide. The cast iron firing piston, shaped like a dumb-bell, fitted tightly into the firing tube and carried a lug which projected up through the slot at the top of the tube; this lug engaged in a U-shaped launching shoe on the underside of the flying bomb.

When it was ready for launching the flying bomb was moved on a special trolley from the assembly hall to the ramp, where it was lowered on to the launching cradle, which had previously been positioned over the lug from the firing piston. The cradle fitted between the guide rails on the firing ramp, its flat wooden underside resting on the smooth greased slideway.

Meanwhile the fuelling squad had made ready the starter trolley, topping up its containers holding the two rocket-type fuels used – hydrogen peroxide (*T Stoff*) and calcium permanganate (*Z Stoff*) – and charging the compressed air cylinders which would be used to pump them. When the starter trolley was loaded, its combustion chamber was plugged into the breech of the firing tube at the base of the ramp.

After the missile's pre-launching checks had been completed, the various squads withdrew to a safe distance from the ramp and the remaining operations were carried out by remote control from the concrete firing bunker.

When all was ready the site commander in the bunker pushed the launching switches. Compressed air was released into the missile's fuel tank to force the petrol up to the motor, the electrical ignition plugs began to spark and the motor started running. Simultaneously, the *T Stoff* and *Z Stoff* were forced by compressed air into the combustion chamber of the starter trolley; the two chemical fuels reacted violently, to produce super-heated steam and oxygen at a rapidly increasing pressure. After starting, the flying bomb's motor ran at partial power for three seconds then at full power for seven seconds. When its thrust, together with the pressure of gases behind the firing piston, became strong enough they caused the shearing of the bolt which held the launching cradle and the missile to the ramp. The flying bomb shot forward, accelerating rapidly.

As the firing piston moved up the firing tube, the pressure of the expanding gases behind it forced a sealing tube into the slot to close it off; this crude seal was not very effective, and a trail of white smoke from the escaping gases followed the missile up the ramp. The flying speed of the Fi 103 was about 190mph; when it reached the end of the launching ramp it was moving at approximately 250mph, and continued away in a steady climb. The launching cradle and the firing piston fell away from the flying bomb as it left the ramp, and dropped to the ground; they would be used again.

The launching crew's part in the firing was now complete, and the above process was repeated. A well-drilled crew could launch one bomb roughly every half hour and there was a case of a single site loosing off eighteen missiles during one night. During any single twenty-four hour period, however, the number of bombs launched by *Flak Regiment 155 (W)* never exceeded three hundred; the average was just over one hundred.

The Flight of the 'Doodle Bug'

Once it was off the ramp the flying bomb climbed at about 500 feet per minute until it reached its previously-set cruising altitude (usually 1,000 metres, about 3,200 feet). Three minutes after launch, when the missile was about half-way through its climb, the auto-pilot began to turn it on to the previously-set heading for its target; this turn was very slow, at a rate of one degree per second. The auto-pilot could cope with pre-set turns of up to 60 degrees from the direction of launch. At a pre-set distance after launch, the air log made the warhead 'live'.

Owing to the wide tolerances used during their construction, the performance of flying bombs varied greatly. They were observed crossing the coast of England at altitudes between tree-top height and 8,000 feet, though most were at between 3,000 and 4,000 feet. Speeds, too, varied considerably. The slowest missiles came in at about 300mph, the fastest at 420mph; the most usual speed was about 350mph. Once the missile levelled off after its climb it continued at an almost constant speed, in spite of the fact that it became lighter as its fuel was burnt; this was because the efficiency of its pulse jet deteriorated with running, as its inlet shutter vanes – which were designed to function for only about 40 minutes – gradually burnt away. On occasions the shutter vanes burned so quickly that the motor ceased to function altogether and the flying bomb would glide to the ground short of the target.

Some Fi 103s carried a simple radio transmitter, which was switched on by the air log when the missile reached a position about 35 miles from the target. At the switch-on point the trailing aerial was released, and streamed back about 450 feet from the rear of the bomb; about half a minute later the set began to transmit. The signal comprised a morse letter for identification followed by a continuous note, repeated twice each minute; this went out on frequencies between 350 and 450 kilocycles. A pair of ground direction-finding stations tracked the missile's flight, and the cross of their bearings when the transmission ceased provided an indication of where the bomb had fallen. Correcting information was then passed to the launching sites, so that the range and bearing of subsequent missiles could be adjusted to allow for the wind.

When the flying bomb arrived at its previously-set target range, the air log fired two detonators in the tail unit. These locked the elevator and the rudder control surfaces, and at the same time released two spoilers under the tailplane which bunted the missile into a steep dive. There was no device to stop the motor at this stage of the flight. But usually the bunt caused the small amount of fuel left in the tank to run to the forward end, and thus uncover the feed pipe; when this happened, the motor cut out.

When the flying bomb struck the ground there were two separate systems to set off its warhead: an electrical impact fuse and a mechanical all-ways impact fuse; also, as a back-up in case the other two failed, there was a clockwork time fuse. In combination these three were so effective that out of the first 2,700 flying bombs to fall on the British Isles, only four failed to explode.

When it exploded, the thinly-cased warhead of 1,870 pounds of high explosive had a somewhat greater blast effect than that of an ordinary bomb of similar weight, because detonation was at ground level rather than slightly below it. The radius of the resultant blast damage varied considerably, but against brick buildings of normal construction was approximately as follows: to a radius of 25 yards, total demolition; to 35 yards, major structural damage; to 55 yards, minor structural damage; beyond a radius of 55 yards, superficial damage such as broken windows and tiles and collapsed ceilings.

The Fieseler 103 Summed Up

In spite of its many clever features, the accuracy of the Fi 103 was in no way comparable to even poorly-aimed bombs from conventional aircraft. The RAF jamming organisation had great sport with the flying-bomb transmissions, with the result that those received were usually quite misleading. Because of this corrections for wind were often based on guesswork; it it was not allowed for, a 30mph side wind could blow a bomb 15 miles off the intended track during a half-hour flight. The overall accuracy of the ground-launched flying bombs over ranges of 120 to 130 miles, discounting the one bomb out of ten that crashed soon after launch, was such that the 50 per cent zone was about *eight miles*; for those bombs fired over ranges of 200 miles, the 50 per cent zone was *twelve miles*. In 1944 the radius of the Greater London built-up area was about six miles; so only one out of eight of the successfully-launched 200-mile-range bombs could reach this largest of targets, even had there been no fighter, gun or balloon defences. From this it can be seen that the Fi 103 could have some effect on morale, but only negligible military value, when used against any sprawling urban area vital to the enemy within about 150 miles of the launching site.

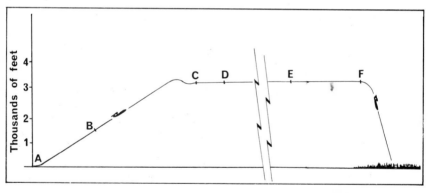

The Flight of the Doodle-Bug. A – after launch, the missile climbed away at 500 feet per minute. B – three minutes after launch it began its turn on to the previously-set heading for the target. C – at the previously-set cruising altitude, the auto-pilot levelled the missile. D – when the flying bomb was safely clear of friendly territory the air log armed the warhead. E – about 35 miles from the target the air log switched on the missile's radio transmitter (if one was fitted). F – at the previously-set target range the air log caused detonators to fire and lock the elevators and rudder; simultaneously, spoilers under the tail plane were released which bunted the missile into a steep dive and held it there until impact.

9
Biographies of Senior Commanders

The ranks stated are those held at the time of death, or at the end of the War.

Reichsmarschall Hermann Wilhelm Goering

Born at Rosenheim in Bavaria on January 12th, 1893. Commissioned as a Leutnant in the Imperial Army in March 1912, he fought as an infantry officer from the beginning of the First World War until October 1914. He then transferred to the Flying Service, and flew initially as an artillery observer. Retrained as a pilot in 1915, he flew reconnaissance operations with the *5. Abteilung* before joining the fighter unit *Jagdstaffel 27*. In May 1918 he received the *Pour le Mérite*, the highest decoration for gallantry, following his twenty-first aerial victory. Two months later he was appointed commander of *Jagdgeschwader* Richthofen, and held that position until the Armistice. Demobilised after the war, he engaged in a series of aviation ventures in Germany and Sweden before joining the new National Socialist Party. In 1923 he played an active part in Hitler's attempted *Putsch* in Munich, and fled to Sweden when it failed. In 1927, following a government amnesty, he returned to Germany and again became active in politics. In May 1928 he was elected to the Reichstag and in 1933, following the formation of the National Socialist government, he received several important posts including that of State Minister for Air. By this time he wielded considerable political power, being second only to Hitler in the Party, and under his aegis the policy of building the secret German air force into a first-rate fighting force received the highest priority in terms of both money and materials. From the public unveiling of the new force in 1935 he held the post of Commander-in-Chief of the *Luftwaffe* and was promoted to Generalfeldmarschall in 1938 and Reichsmarschall in 1940. After the beginning of the war, however, his many other assumed duties in the Third Reich, as well as his frequent and progressively more lengthy periods of leave, meant that he devoted little of his time to the actual running of the air force; and when he did intervene his influence was often harmful. With the general deterioration of the fighting ability of the *Luftwaffe* after the beginning of 1943, Goering's personal position declined steadily. Finally, following an unsuccessful attempt to take over power from Hitler, he was dismissed from all his posts on April 23rd, 1945. After the war he was tried at Nuremburg on charges of conspiracy, crimes against peace, general war crimes and crimes against humanity; convicted of all four, he was sentenced to death by hanging. Before this sentence could be carried out, he committed suicide by taking poison on October 15th, 1946.*

Generalfeldmarschall Robert, Ritter von Greim

Born in 1892, he entered the Royal Bavarian Army as a cadet in 1911. During the early part of the First World War he served in the artillery, before transfering to the Flying Service in 1916. He became a successful fighter pilot and rose to command *Jagdstaffel 34* and later *Jagdgruppe 10*; at the end of the war he was credited with 28 aerial victories and held the *Pour le Mérite*. Following the Armistice he went to China, where he helped organise an air force for General Chiang Kai-shek, then returned to Germany where he started a school for commercial pilots. During the secret rebuilding of the *Luftwaffe* he took command of the re-formed Richthofen *Geschwader*. In April 1935 he was appointed to the post of Inspector of Fighters and Dive Bombers, in the following year became the Inspector of Equipment and Flight Safety, and in 1937 was made head of the Personnel Section of the Air Ministry. In 1939 he moved to command *Fliegerdivision 5* (later re-designated *Fliegerkorps V*) and held this post during the campaign in Flanders, the Battle of Britain and the invasion of Russia. He was still in command when *Fliegerkorps V* was re-named *Luftwaffe* Command East, in April 1942, and also when it subsequently became *Luftflotte 6*, in July 1943; he was promoted to Generaloberst in February 1943. In April 1945 he was promoted to Generalfeldmarschall and replaced Goering as Commander-in-Chief of what was left of the *Luftwaffe*. In June 1945, shortly after being taken prisoner, he committed suicide.

Generalfeldmarschall Albert Kesselring

Born in 1895, he entered the Imperial Army in 1914 and served as a Brigade Adjutant and General Staff officer during the First World War. After the Armistice he remained in the army. In October 1933 he transferred to the new *Luftwaffe* and became head of the Administration Office. In 1934 he was promoted to General and for a short period from the middle of 1936 he held the post of Chief of the General Staff of the *Luftwaffe*. In 1938 he assumed command of *Luftwaffengruppe 1*. At the outbreak of the Second World War he was in command of *Luftflotte 1* in Poland, and early in 1940 he moved to take charge of *Luftflotte 2*, which he led during the operations in the west and from the beginning of the campaign in Russia. In December 1941 *Luftflotte 2* moved to the Mediterranean; Kesselring remained in command and in addition was appointed C. in C. of all German forces in the area. In 1943 he gave up his command of *Luftflotte 2* but remained as C. in C. South in command of the German forces in Italy until March 1945, when he became C. in C. West. He died in 1960.†

* Biography: 'Hermann Goering' by Asher Lee.

† Autobiography: 'The Memoirs of Field Marshal Kesselring', published in Britain by William Kimber Ltd.

Above: Hermann Goering, right, was the Commander-in-Chief of the *Luftwaffe* from the beginning of its secret expansion in 1933 until just before the close of the Second World War. At the time this picture was taken, in the spring of 1939, he held the rank of Generalfeldmarschall. He is seen welcoming Generalmajor (as he then was) Wolfram von Richthofen back to Germany following the conclusion of the Spanish civil war.

Right: Generalfeldmarschall Robert, Ritter von Greim./*IWM*

Left: Generalfeldmarschall Albert Kesselring (right) pictured with General der Flieger (at the time this picture was taken) Hans Jeschonnek.

Below left: Generalfeldmarschall Erhard Milch./*IWM*

Below: Generalfeldmarschall Hugo Sperrle./*IWM*

Generalfeldmarschall Erhard Milch

Born in 1892, he was commissioned into an artillery regiment in the Imperial Army in 1909. Following active service on the eastern front against the Russians he transferred to the Flying Service in 1915 and for most of the remainder of the war he flew on reconnaissance operations. After the war he entered business, and in 1926 became the Director of the airline *Deutsche Lufthansa*. In 1933 he was appointed to the post of State Secretary for Aviation, and in this position he played a major part in the building up of the German aircraft industry so that it could provide aircraft in the numbers needed for the rapidly-expanding *Luftwaffe*. In 1936 he was promoted to General der Flieger and in 1938 to Generaloberst; in 1940 he became a Generalfeldmarschall. Following the suicide of Ernst Udet in November 1941, Milch took over the post of Director General of Equipment in addition to his other duties. In the years that followed, however, relations between Milch and Goering became increasingly bitter. Finally, following a stormy meeting with Hitler in May 1944, when the latter insisted on having the Messerschmitt 262 jet aircraft produced as a fighter-bomber instead of a fighter, Milch was stripped of his powers. After the war he was tried and convicted for his part in the forced transportation of foreign workers to Germany and sentenced to life imprisonment; later this was reduced to fifteen years, and he was released on parole in 1955. He died in January 1972.*

Generalfeldmarschall Dr Ing. Wolfram Freiherr von Richthofen

Born in 1895, he was commissioned into a Hussar regiment of the Imperial Army in 1913. He transferred to the Flying Service in 1917 and served as a pilot in *Jagdgeschwader* Richthofen (named after his late cousin, Manfred); when the war ended he had been credited with 8 victories. After the Armistice he left the service to study engineering, and received his doctorate before rejoining the *Reichswehr* in 1923. In 1933 he transferred to the new *Luftwaffe* and was employed in the Air Ministry. In November 1936 he was appointed the first commander of the small German expeditionary air force sent to Spain; two years later he returned there to head the by now greatly expanded *Legion Kondor*. During the Polish, Flanders, Balkan and Russian campaigns he commanded *Fliegerkorps VIII*, and in this post he built his reputation as one of the most successful exponents of intensive close support air operations, using the Junkers 87 dive bomber. In July 1942 he took command of *Luftflotte 4*; and a year later he was promoted Generalfeldmarschall and moved to command *Luftflotte 2* in the Mediterranean area. In November 1944 he contacted a brain tumour and was transferred to the reserve, and in July the following year he died.

Generalfeldmarschall Hugo Sperrle

Born in 1885, he joined an infantry regiment in the Imperial Army in 1903. He served in the Flying Service during the First World War, and rose to command

* Biography 'The Rise and Fall of the Luftwaffe – The Life of Erhard Milch' by David Irving, published in Britain by Weidenfeld & Nicolson.

Left: Generaloberst Guenter Korten.

Below: Generaloberst Ernst Udet (left) speaking to Oberstleutnant (later Generalleutnant) Adolf Galland (centre) on the right is the fighter ace Oberst Werner Moelders / *via Schliephake*

the flying units attached to the 7th Army. After the war he remained in the *Reichswehr* and transferred to the *Luftwaffe* in 1935. Following a short period in command of the *Legion Kondor* in Spain he moved, early in 1938, to command *Luftwaffengruppe 3* and remained in this position when it was later renamed *Luftflotte 3*. He commanded the *Luftflotte* during the Flanders campaign and the Battle of Britain, and the spasmodic air operations against Britain afterwards. In August 1944, at the age of 59, he was transferred to the reserve.

Generaloberst Hans Jeschonnek

Born in 1899, he entered the Imperial Army in 1914 as a cadet infantry officer. In 1917 he transferred to the Flying Service and fought as a fighter pilot with *Jagdstaffel 40*. After the Armistice he remained in the *Reichswehr* as a cavalry officer. In 1933 he transferred to the new *Luftwaffe* as a staff officer with the rank of Hauptmann, to begin a meteoric career which within six years took him to the position of Chief of the General Staff of the *Luftwaffe*, with the rank of Generalmajor. In 1940 his abilities were further rewarded when he was promoted direct to General der Flieger without serving in the intermediate rank of Generalleutnant. During the years of victory he was held in high esteem and in March 1942 he was promoted to Generaloberst. By the middle of 1943, however, the *Luftwaffe* was beginning to lose control of events and was failing in its purpose as a fighting service. The primary reason for this was the massive Allied superiority in resources, but both Hitler and Goering made it clear to Jeschonnek that they held him personally responsible for the deterioration of the *Luftwaffe*. On August 19th, 1943 he did what was expected of him, and committed suicide by shooting.

Generaloberst Guenther Korten

Born in 1898, he joined an artillery regiment of the Imperial Army as an officer cadet in 1914. During the First World War he served in the army, and remained with the *Reichswehr* afterwards. In 1934 he transferred to the *Luftwaffe*, and by 1939 he was Chief of Staff of *Luftflotte 4* during the Polish campaign. During the Flanders campaign he served as Chief of Staff of *Luftflotte 3*; the following year he returned to *Luftflotte 4*, holding this same position during the Balkans campaign and the early stages of that in Russia. In August 1942 he was appointed to head *Luftwaffe* Command Don, with the rank of Generalleutnant; in January the following year he was promoted to General der Flieger. In June 1943 he was made commander of *Luftflotte 1* in Russia but held this post for only a short time for in September, following the suicide of Jeschonnek, he became the Chief of the General Staff of the *Luftwaffe*. Korten received severe injuries during the attempt on Hitler's life on July 20th, 1944, and died a few days later.

Generaloberst Hans Juergen Stumpff

Born in 1890, he entered the Imperial Army in 1907. During the First World War he served as an infantry officer until 1916, when he was appointed to the General Staff. After the Armistice he remained with the *Reichswehr* and in 1933 he transferred to the *Luftwaffe* as Chief of the Personnel Office. From June 1937 until January 1939 he was Chief of the General Staff of the *Luftwaffe*, with the rank of Generalleutnant. During the early part of 1940 he commanded *Luftflotte 1* then, following his promotion to Generaloberst in May, he took command of *Luftflotte 5* in Norway and Finland; he remained in this position until November 1943. Early in 1944 he moved to command *Luftflotte Reich*, responsible for home air defence; he remained in this important post until the end of the war.

Generaloberst Ernst Udet

Born in 1896, he joined the Imperial Army shortly after the outbreak of the First World War. In 1915 he entered the Flying Service and trained as a pilot. In April 1918, following his twentieth aerial victory, he received the Pour le Mérite. At the end of the war his victory total stood at 62 and he was the highest-scoring German pilot to survive the conflict. After the war he achieved international fame as a test, sports and aerobatic pilot. In 1935 he entered the new *Luftwaffe* and early the following year was appointed Inspector of Fighters and Dive-bombers. In June 1936 he became the Director of the Technical Department at the Air Ministry, and in February 1939 was appointed to the post of Director General of Equipment with the rank of Generalleutnant; in July 1940 he was promoted to Generaloberst. But it was clear that his brilliance as a pilot in no way fitted him for the vitally important task of organising the production of aircraft for the *Luftwaffe*; one by one his successive and sometimes conflicting production programmes ran into difficulties. During the early months of the Russian campaign the *Luftwaffe* suffered heavy losses in aircraft and when their replacements were not forthcoming the failure of Udet's office became clear. Udet himself suffered from increasingly serious bouts of depression and on November 17th, 1941 he shot himself.*

General der Flieger Josef Kammhuber

Born in 1896, he entered the Imperial Army in 1914, serving first in a Pioneer battalion and later in the infantry. He continued in the army throughout the First World War, and remained with the *Reichswehr* afterwards. In 1933 he transferred to the *Luftwaffe* and was initially employed as a staff officer at the Air Ministry. During the Flanders campaign he served as *Kommodore* of *Kampfgeschwader 51*; he was shot down by the French and taken prisoner, but freed after the armistice. In the summer of 1940 he held the rank of Oberst, and received orders to organise a night fighter force to counter the RAF attacks on targets in Germany; by the middle of 1941 this had become *Fliegerkorps XII* and by the end of the year Kammhuber had been promoted to Generalleutnant. The night fighter force expanded steadily to keep pace with the strengthening RAF attacks, and by the beginning of 1943 Kammhuber's *Fliegerkorps* was one of the most important in the *Luftwaffe*; in January of that year he was promoted to General der Flieger. In July 1943, however, the radar close-controlled night fighting methods pioneered by Kammhuber were rendered ineffective by the large-scale release of 'Window' metal foil from the RAF bombers; with the demise of his system, Kammhuber fell rapidly from favour. From November

* Biography: 'Udet – A Man's Life' by Hans Herlin, published in Britain by Macdonald.

1943 to February 1945 he commanded the less important *Luftflotte 5* in Norway and Finland. He returned to favour only at the end of the war, when during the final three months he was appointed as Goering's Special Plenipotentiary for jet and rocket aircraft. In 1956 he joined the *Bundeswehr* and became Inspector of the re-formed *Luftwaffe*; he held this post until 1962, when he retired.

General der Flieger Karl Koller

Born in 1898, he entered the Imperial Army in 1914; in 1917 he transferred to the Flying Service and trained as pilot. After the war he served with the Bavarian Police Force until 1935, when he joined the *Luftwaffe*. In 1938 he became head of the operations staff of *Luftwaffengruppe 3* (soon afterwards re-named *Luftflotte 3*) and in January 1941 he became its Chief of Staff. In September 1943 he was appointed head of the *Luftwaffe* Operations Staff. In November 1944 he became the Chief of the General Staff of the *Luftwaffe* in succession to Kreipe, and remained in this post until the end of the war.

General der Flieger Werner Kreipe

Born in 1904, he entered the *Reichswehr* in 1922. The following November, while attending the Military Academy in Munich, he took part in the abortive National Socialist *Putsch*. In 1930 he underwent flying training and in 1934 transferred from the army to the new *Luftwaffe* with the rank of Hauptmann. He served as a liaison officer with the Italian Air Force in 1936, and in a similar role with the Belgian Air Force in 1937. In 1940 he was appointed *Kommodore* of *Kampfgeschwader 2* in France; the following year he became Chief of Staff of *Fliegerkorps I* in Russia. In July 1943 he was appointed to the post of General in charge of training. From August to November 1944 he filled the post of Chief of the General Staff of the *Luftwaffe*, following the death of Korten. During the final six months of the war he was Commandant of the Air Warfare College at Berlin. After the war he served with the Federal Ministry of Traffic in Bonn.

Generalleutnant Adolf Galland

Born in 1912, he began his flying training in 1932 at a school for airline pilots. In 1934 he entered the *Luftwaffe* and in November was commissioned as a Leutnant. Between May 1937 and June 1938 he commanded the *3rd Staffel* of *Jagdgruppe 88*, operating Heinkel 51s in Spain. During the Polish campaign he flew Henschel 123s in the ground attack role, commanding a *Staffel* of *II (Schlacht) LG 2*. By June 1940 he held the rank of Hauptmann and was appointed to command the fighter unit *III./JG26*, with which he fought during the Flanders campaign. Promoted to Major in July, the following month he assumed command of *Jagdgeschwader 26* and led the unit during the Battle of Britain; also in August, following his seventeenth victory, he received the Ritterkreuz. His success as a fighter pilot brought him a steady stream of decorations: in September 1940, after forty victories, the Oakleaves; in June 1941, following his 69th victory, the Swords; and in January 1942, after 94 victories, he held the Ritterkreuz with Oakleaves, Swords and Diamonds. Following the death of Oberst Moelders, in November 1941, Galland was appointed General in charge of fighters, initially with the rank of Oberst. In November 1942, at the age of thirty, he was promoted to Generalmajor and thus became the youngest officer to attain General rank in the German armed forces. With the *Luftwaffe* steadily being forced on to the defensive, and with the ineffectiveness of the re-equipment and training programmes, Galland's outspoken criticism of the High Command brought him into conflict with Goering. Finally, in January 1945, he was relieved of all Staff duties by Goering; the latter made no objection when Galland put himself in command of the elite Messerschmitt 262 unit *Jagdverband 44*, and led it in action during the closing months of the war. At the close of the conflict Galland's victory total stood at 104.*

* Autobiography: 'The First and the Last', published in Britain by Methuen.

Aircraft Unit Identification Markings

The subject of *Luftwaffe* aircraft unit identification markings is a complex one and the intention in this Appendix is to provide only the general ground rules.

General System of Identification

During the Second World War most *Luftwaffe* front-line aircraft, other than those belonging to single-engined day fighter or ground attack units, carried a code of three letters and one number on their rear fuselage. For example, the Messerschmitt 110s in the photograph overleaf had the fuselage markings 3U + HR and 3U + AR. 3U to the left of the cross was the code of *Zestoerergeschwader 26*. The R on the right was the code letter indicating 7. *Staffel*, which also meant that the aircraft belonged to the *III. Gruppe*; A and H were the identification letters of the individual aircraft within that *Staffel*.

A list of the code letters of the more important *Geschwader* and independent *Gruppen* and *Staffeln* is given below:

A1	*Kampfgeschwader 53*
A2	*Zerstoerergeschwader 52*
A3	*Kampfgeschwader 200*
A5	*Stukageschwader 1*
A6	*Aufklaerungsgruppe 120*
B3	*Kampfgeschwader 54*
C8	*Transportgeschwader 5*
C9	*Nachtjagdgeschwader 5*
D1	*Seeaufklaerungsgruppe 126*
D5	*Nachtjagdgeschwader 3*
F1	*Kampfgeschwader 76*
F1	*Stukageschwader 76*
F6	*Aufklaerungsgruppe 122*
F7	*Seeaufklaerungsgruppe 130*
F8	*Kampfgeschwader 40*
G1	*Kampfgeschwader 55*

G2	*Aufklaerungsgruppe 124*
G6	*Kampfgeschwader z.b.V 2**
G6	*Transportgeschwader 4*
G9	*Nachtjagdgeschwader 1*
H1	*Aufklaerungsgruppe 12*
J4	*Transportstaffel 5*
J9	*Stukageschwader 5*
K6	*Kuestenfliegergruppe 406*
K7	*Nachtaufklaerungsgruppe*
L1	*Lehrgeschwader 1*
L2	*Lehrgeschwader 2*
L5	*Kampfgruppe z.b.V. 5*
M2	*Kuestenfliegergruppe 106*
M2	*Kampfgruppe 106*
M7	*Kampfgruppe 806*
M8	*Zerstoerergeschwader 76*
P1	*Kampfgeschwader 60*
P2	*Aufklaerungsgruppe 21*
R4	*Nachtjagdgeschwader 2*
S2	*Stukageschwader 77*
S3	*Transportgruppe 30*
S4	*Kuestenfliegergruppe 506*
S4	*Kampfgruppe 506*
S7	*Stukageschwader 3*
S9	*Schnellkampfgeschwader 210*
T1	*Aufklaerungsgruppe 10*
T6	*Stukageschwader 2*
U5	*Kampfgeschwader 2*
U8	*Zerstoerergeschwader 26*
V4	*Kampfgeschwader 1*
V7	*Aufklaerungsgruppe 32*
W7	*Nachtjagdgeschwader 100*
Z6	*Kampfgeschwader 66*
1G	*Kampfgeschwader 27*
1H	*Kampfgeschwader 26*
1K	*Nachtschlachtgruppe 4*
1T	*Kampfgruppe 126*
1T	*Kampfgeschwader 28*
1Z	*Kampfgeschwader z.b.V. 1*
1Z	*Transportgeschwader 1*
2J	*Zerstoerergeschwader 1*
2N	*Zerstoerergeschwader 76*
2S	*Zerstoerergeschwader 2*
2Z	*Nachtjagdgeschwader 6*
3C	*Nachtjagdgeschwader 4*

* *z.b.V. – zur besonderen Verwendung*, meaning 'for special purpose'. This designation in fact referred to transport units early in the war. Later these were re-designated *Transportgeschwader*.

Top: Messerschmitt 110s of the *7Staffel* of *ZG26*. The unit identification markings are explained in the text.

Above: Dornier 17 reconnaissance aircraft, carrying the 4N code of *Aufklaerungsgruppe 22./via Obert*

3E	*Kampfgeschwader 6*
3K	*Minesuchsgruppe*
3M	*Zerstoerergeschwader 2*
3U	*Zerstoerergeschwader 26*
3W	*Nachtschlachtgruppe 11*
3Z	*Kampfgeschwader 77*
4D	*Kampfgeschwader 30*
4N	*Aufklaerungsgruppe 22*
4R	*Nachtjagdgeschwader 2*
4U	*Aufklaerungsgruppe 123*
4V	*Kampfgruppe z.b.V. 172*
4V	*Transportgeschwader 3*
5D	*Aufklaerungsgruppe 31*
5F	*Aufklaerungsgruppe 14*
5J	*Kampfgeschwader 4*
5K	*Kampfgeschwader 3*
6G	*Stukageschwader 51*
6I	*Kuestenfliegergruppe 706*
6N	*Kampfgruppe 100*
6N	*Kampfgeschwader 100*
6R	*Seeaufklaerungsgruppe 127*
6U	*Zerstoerergeschwader 1*
6W	*Seeaufklaerungsgruppe 128*
7A	*Aufklaerungsgruppe 121*
7J	*Nachtjagdgeschwader 102*
7R	*Seeaufklaerungsgruppe 125*
7T	*Kampfgruppe 606*
7V	*Kampfgruppe z.b.V 700*
8H	*Aufklaerungsgruppe 33*
8L	*Kuestenfliegergruppe 906*
8T	*Kampfgruppe z.b.V. 800*
8T	*Transportgeschwader 2*
9K	*Kampfgeschwader 51*
9P	*Kampfgruppe z.b.V. 9*
9V	*Fernaufklaerungsgruppe 5*
9W	*Nachtjagdgeschwader 101*

As has been mentioned, the final letter of the identification code denoted the *Staffel* (or *Stab*) to which the aircraft belonged. The full list of *Stab* and *Staffel* identification letters is as follows:

A	*Geschwader Stab*
B	*I. Gruppe Stab*
C	*II. Gruppe Stab*
D	*III. Gruppe Stab*
E	*IV. Gruppe Stab*
F	*V. Gruppe Stab*
H	*1. Staffel (I. Gruppe)*

K	2. Staffel (I. Gruppe)
L	3. Staffel (I. Gruppe)
M	4. Staffel (II. Gruppe)
N	5. Staffel (II. Gruppe)
P	6. Staffel (II. Gruppe)
R	7. Staffel (III. Gruppe)
S	8. Staffel (III. Gruppe)
T	9. Staffel (III. Gruppe)
U	10. Staffel (IV. Gruppe)
V	11. Staffel (IV. Gruppe)
W	12. Staffel (IV. Gruppe)
X	13. Staffel (V. Gruppe)
Y	14. Staffel (V. Gruppe)
Z	15. Staffel (V. Gruppe)

In addition to the three letter code and rear fuselage number operational aircraft often carried a *Geschwader*, *Gruppe* or *Staffel* badge, usually on the nose.

Identification Markings carried by Single-engined Day Fighter or Ground Attack Aircraft

The system of unit identification markings applied to German single-engined day fighter and ground attack aircraft (but *not* dive-bombers) differed markedly from that applied to other types of aircraft. There was no simple letter-and-number code denoting *Geschwader*, *Gruppe* and *Staffel*; instead, until almost the end of the war, this was denoted only by the individual *Geschwader*, *Gruppe* or *Staffel* badge applied to the nose or rear fuselage (sometimes even this was omitted, so that the aircraft bore no *Geschwader* identification).

Within the *Geschwader*, the aircraft of the individual *Gruppen* were identified by the symbol to the rear of the fuselage cross, as follows: *I. Gruppe*, no marking; *II. Gruppe*, a horizontal bar; *III. Gruppe*, a wavy line *or* a vertical bar; *IV. Gruppe*, a circle *or* a cross.

Forward of the fuselage cross fighter and ground attack aircraft usually carried a number between 1 and 16, to identify the aircraft within its *Staffel*. In place of this identifying number, the aircraft flown by officers holding executive positions with *Geschwader* or *Gruppe* staffs carried identifying chevrons, bars and/or circles as follows:

On February 20th 1945, almost at the end of the war, the day fighter units engaged in the defence of the Reich (at that time almost all of the day fighter units remaining operational) began carrying coloured bands round the rear fuselage to identify their *Geschwader*; a complete list of these is given opposite.

German day fighter units sometimes painted part or all of the motor cowlings of their aircraft in distinctive colours (yellow, white or red), or with distinctive designs (black and white stripes, checks etc) to ease identification in combat. Such markings were not often used and they did not constitute any form of permanent unit identification; despite copious Allied reports to the contrary, they did *not* denote that the aircraft bearing them belonged to 'crack' units.

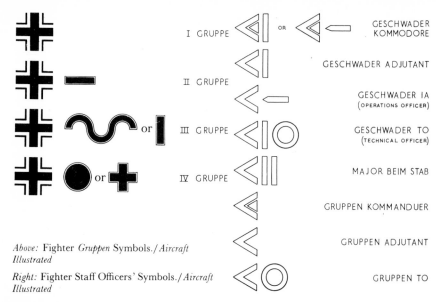

I GRUPPE

II GRUPPE

or

III GRUPPE

or

IV GRUPPE

GESCHWADER KOMMODORE

GESCHWADER ADJUTANT

GESCHWADER IA
(OPERATIONS OFFICER)

GESCHWADER TO
(TECHNICAL OFFICER)

MAJOR BEIM STAB

GRUPPEN KOMMANDUER

GRUPPEN ADJUTANT

GRUPPEN TO

Above: Fighter *Gruppen* Symbols./*Aircraft Illustrated*

Right: Fighter Staff Officers' Symbols./*Aircraft Illustrated*

Above: A Messerschmitt 109F, carrying on its nose the Cockerel's Head insignia of *III.Gruppe* of *Jagdgeschwader 2*. The vertical strip on the rear fuselage confirms that the aircraft belongs to *III.Gruppe* and the chevrons in front of the fuselage cross indicate that it was flown by the *Gruppen Kommandeur*./*via RC Seeley*

Right: Geschwader identification markings, carried by aircraft of German fighter units after February 20th, 1945.

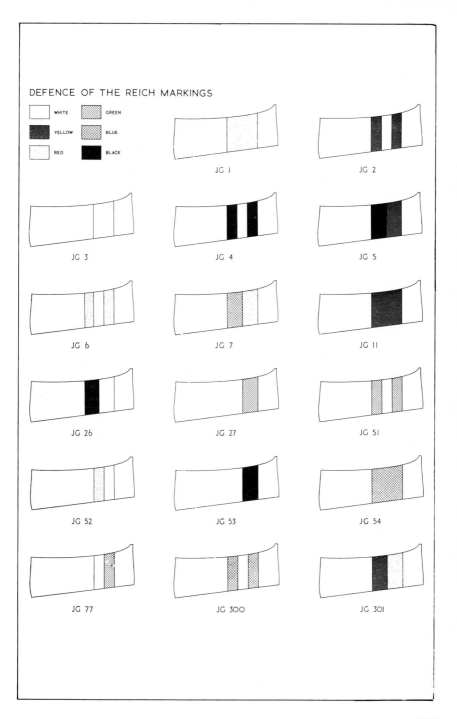

DEFENCE OF THE REICH MARKINGS

WHITE   GREEN
YELLOW   BLUE
RED   BLACK

JG 1   JG 2

JG 3   JG 4   JG 5

JG 6   JG 7   JG 11

JG 26   JG 27   JG 51

JG 52   JG 53   JG 54

JG 77   JG 300   JG 301

APPENDIX B
Rank Insignia

The list below gives equivalent wartime ranks in the RAF and USAAF.

	Luftwaffe	*Royal Air Force*	*US Army Air Force*
1	Generalfeldmarschall	Marshal of the Royal Air Force	General (five star)
2	Generaloberst	Air Chief Marshal	General (four star)
3	General der Flieger	Air Marshal	Lieutenant General
4	Generalleutnant	Air Vice Marshal	Major General
5	Generalmajor	Air Commodore	Brigadier General
6	Oberst	Group Captain	Colonel
7	Oberstleutnant	Wing Commander	Lieutenant Colonel
8	Major	Squadron Leader	Major
9	Hauptmann	Flight Lieutenant	Captain
10	Oberleutnant	Flying Officer	First Lieutenant
11	Leutnant	Pilot Officer	Lieutenant
12	Stabsfeldwebel	Warrant Officer	Warrant Officer
13	Oberfeldwebel	Flight Sergeant	Master Sergeant
14	Feldwebel	Sergeant	Technical Sergeant
15	Unterfeldwebel	—	—
16	Unteroffizier	Corporal	Staff Sergeant
17	Hauptgefreiter	—	Sergeant
18	Obergefreiter	Leading Aircraftman	Corporal
19	Gefreiter	Aircraftman First Class	Private First Class
20	Flieger	Aircraftman Second Class	Private

Right: Rank Insignia.

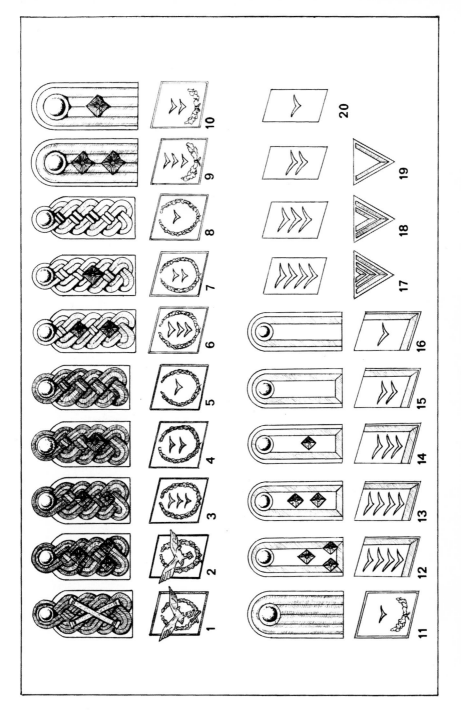

Above/Right: The night fighter ace Helmut Lent, pictured wearing the decorations he held in the summer of 1944. He was killed in a flying accident the following October, credited with 102 night and 8 day victories. (*1*) collar tabs and epaulets of an Oberstleutnant. (*2*) standard *Luftwaffe* eagle (worn by all ranks). (*3*) pilot's wings (*4*) Ritterkreuz with oak leaves, swords and diamonds. (*5*) Deutsche Kreuz. (*6*) Iron Cross first class. (*7*) Mission Clasp, with additional pennant for more than 250 operational night fighter sorties. (*8*) wound badge. (*9*) Narvik Shield, worn by those who had taken part in the battles to capture the Norwegian port. (*10*) Junior officer's summer hat.